Advance Praise for

READY FOR ANYTHING by David

"In fifty-two short chapters, David Allen shares his principles for 'mastering the game of work and the business of life.' No one makes the challenges of productivity more understandable and manageable."

—*Rob Johnston, President, Leader to Leader Institute*

"David's unique mix of wisdom, smarts, experience, and tools gives you everything you might need to get your life back—no one should make it back to work next Monday morning without having devoured this brilliant book."

—*Ben Cannon, Partner, Heidrick & Struggles; former head of Learning and Professional Development, Goldman Sachs*

"In the pages of *Ready for Anything*, you come to realize that managing your time has little to do with lists, regimen, or rigid systems. Rather, it's about learning how to aspire to great things and to tap in to that purpose, with as much energy and focus as a given moment allows. This fundamentally different look at productivity makes David's book not just a good read, but also something you can truly live by."

—*Keith Yamashita, Principal, Stone Yamashita Partners*

"What a stimulating dose of uncommon sense! These powerful and practical pointers for living a more productive life are as subtle and rich as they are simple. David Allen is a master at marrying the sensible with the sublime."

—*Arianna Huffington*

Ready
for
Anything

Also by David Allen

Getting Things Done: The Art of Stress-Free Productivity

Ready for Anything

52 Productivity Principles for Work and Life

DAVID ALLEN

piatkus

PIATKUS

First published in the US in 2003 by Penguin Group
First published in Great Britain in 2004 by Piatkus
This paperback edition published in 2011 by Piatkus

A CIP catalogue record for this book
is available from the British Library.

ISBN 978-0-7499-4102-4

Printed and bound by CPI Group (UK) Ltd, Croydon, CR0 4YY

Papers used by Piatkus are natural, renewable and
recyclable products sourced from well-managed forests and certified
in accordance with the rules of the Forest Stewardship Council.

MIX
Paper from
responsible sources
FSC® C104740

Piatkus
An imprint of
Little, Brown Book Group
100 Victoria Embankment
London EC4Y 0DY

An Hachette UK Company
www.hachette.co.uk

www.piatkus.co.uk

To all who've taught me to learn and grow,
whether they've known it or not

Acknowledgments

MAJOR THANKS are due Stephen Singular, a freelance editor and fellow author, whom we tasked to review the last six years of my writings to distill themes and create an initial structure. His energetic, timely efforts and feedback provided a critical "stake in the ground" that allowed me to sharpen the focus, format the context, and really get going on this work.

Much of the material herein was originally published on my Web site and then through my e-newsletters, and as such would not have been realized as easily without the technical expertise of Greg Fisk and Eric Mack, nor without the tireless support of our office staff—especially Jodi Womack. And I'm so grateful that Steve Shull early on inspired me with the idea of a newsletter as a significant platform from which to share my material.

Thanks (nicely, now, "as usual") to my editor at Viking, Janet Goldstein, whose encouragement, insights, and hustle were catalytic. And to my agent, Doe Coover, who captained the project.

My wife, Kathryn, has been the backbone of the business that has allowed me to produce this material, and she's provided me not only her love but also the demonstration of it in the vital support and healthy nudges I needed, when I've most needed them.

Contents

PART V: REMIND YOURSELF OF THE FUNDAMENTALS
or Common Sense Isn't That Common   155

MAXIMUM PRODUCTIVITY is making something happen—furniture, freeways, or fun—with as little *effort* as possible. The fact that we have "effort" at all, though, implies that we confront resistance and impediments when we want to get anything done. Improving productivity has a lot to do with dealing more effectively with the hindrances, barriers, and distractions that show up in our way— anything that opposes or weakens our forward motion. In a totally frictionless world, everything would just appear as soon as it was imagined—there would be little need to train for greater flexibility and focus or to install better systems and approaches. In the world you and I inhabit, however, to really get what we want most effectively, we have to be ready for anything. And there *are* things we can all do, anytime, that make it easier to take things in stride and stay the course.

I've spent more than two decades exploring the best methods to achieve a more relaxed, positive, and sustainable way to live and work. And as a management consultant and productivity coach, I've helped thousands of professionals implement what I've discovered to be the best ways to work more productively *and* get more enjoyment from what they're doing. When people gain a method of achieving that kind of balance in their day-to-day endeavors, no matter what's going on, they have easier access to more of their intuition and creativity. They become better at processing information, managing their thoughts and feelings, focusing on results, and trusting their judgments about what to do next. They have a *systematic approach* in place for dealing with themselves and their work, which is far more useful than merely relying on ad hoc, reactive behaviors to bail them out of the pressures and crises of their world. When people know they have a process in place to handle any situation, they are more relaxed. When they're relaxed, everything improves. More gets done, with less effort, and a host of other wonderful side effects emerge that add to the outcomes of their efforts and the quality of their life.

The methods I teach came from the behaviors and the systems I discovered that worked the best to keep us *at* our best. Since the early 1980s, they have been tested and proven highly effective, from the ground up—for both individuals and organizations. The steps of this discovery and this process were described in my first book, *Getting Things Done: The Art of Stress-Free Productivity.* Its success around the world indicated that people across a wide spectrum of cultures and careers seemed ready for this information and eager for change. They were tired of feeling overwhelmed by their jobs and the business of life. They wanted to regain lost opportunities for creative thinking and playing. They were looking for a new approach, a *system* that could be counted on, no matter what kind of job they had or what kind of day they were having. They wanted a structure— but a natural one that matched their complex lifestyles and created more freedom, not more constraint.

While I was uncovering and implementing the details of the what, when, and how that made up the heart of my programs, I started doing something else: I began writing about the *why* behind these steps. Why did they work so well? Why did they consistently help people function at a higher capacity and feel better? Was something deeper at work here? What was the foundation behind this success? There seemed to be underlying principles that wove themselves in and through the methodology—factors that held true no matter when, where, or with whom they were applied.

A person can be an excellent race-car driver without knowing anything about gravity, even though gravity is the underlying force affecting everything one does behind the wheel. To win races, the driver needs only to master the steering, the speed on the straight-aways, and the technique of the turns, and to remember to keep the car under control at all times. You do your job, and gravity will do its job. Manage yourself, and the automobile will be fine. But what if driving fast isn't enough after a while? What if you want to know more about why your skills work so well and how they keep you from crashing and burning? What if you want to get closer to the secrets behind your own successes? And what if understanding those secrets leads to more tools for productivity and even greater achievements?

In 1997, I began exploring these questions by compiling a set of principles that seemed to lie at the foundation of productive behav-ior and writing informal essays about the implications and applica-tions of those truths in everyday life. I started to enlarge on my core premise that one's ability to be productive was directly proportional to one's ability to relax. I dug further into four main areas of pro-ductive behavior:

1. Capturing and corralling all our internal and external "open loops" to regain clarity and energy.
2. Consciously managing our focus within the multiple levels of outcomes and responsibilities to which we are committed.
3. Creating trusted structures and consistent usage of them to trigger the appropriate focus and reminders as necessary.
4. Grounding it all with flexible, forward motion at the physical-action level.

I discovered that people didn't need more discipline as such—they needed a disciplined approach. They didn't need to work harder—they needed to define their work better at multiple levels of detail and stay focused on all of them simultaneously.

Behind all this lay the "mind like water" concept, an image I'd come across years ago while studying karate. When you throw a pebble into a pond, what does the water do? It responds with total appropriateness to the force and mass of the rock. It does nothing more and nothing less. It doesn't overreact or underreact. It doesn't react at all. It simply interacts with whatever comes to it and then returns to its natural state. The water can do that only by design. A human being can act this way only if he or she has a conscious system in place and if that system is built on principles that can withstand chaos and stress. Those principles must be aligned with something deeper in our nature.

Two years after I began writing the essays, I decided to write and distribute a newsletter to those who were becoming familiar with my methods. My hope was to galvanize a network of practitioners and to build a community of people dedicated to doing good work, sharing their best practices, and celebrating life. Each newsletter was intended to reinforce and expand the ideas behind relaxed control and performance excellence. I wondered if people would respond.

My answer soon exceeded my expectations. Within two years, our readership had grown tenfold, from two thousand to twenty thousand subscribers. A year later it had reached thirty thousand and was still gathering momentum. People were sending out the newsletters through their own online networks. They were being e-mailed across the country and around the globe. Other folks were printing, stapling, and binding hard copies and distributing them to their friends and colleagues. Still others were posting them in elevators at work. They were showing up everywhere. Some of the essays leaned more toward practical advice, and others delved below the surface. All were developing and growing my understanding of the "why," and all were adding value to what had come before.

The feedback was overwhelmingly positive—people seemed hungry for reinforcement of the basics, exploration of the subtleties, and the adventure of the surprises produced by some of the simplest techniques, tools, and awarenesses. These were hardly people in the Remedial Living class either—the most profound rewards from using this material have been reported by some of the best and brightest people on the planet, many already in the top percentiles of productivity, by anyone's standards.

It was time to put this material together into a book of its own.

The following principles, commentaries, and essays form a body of thought that I believe offers more than just tips or tricks. Whether or not people implemented the complete method of best practices I delineated in *Getting Things Done,* there were still things everyone could do more and more consistently, anytime, that would improve their productivity and well-being. These are the elements you will find validated and reinforced in these principles and essays.

The writings have been sorted into the four major areas of productive behavior they support: completion, focus, structure, and action. The principles and essays grouped as such are meant not to be limited to these headings or to give an exhaustive exposition of those topics but rather to stimulate your own thinking and validations of better ways to handle things.

There are times when individuals (and groups) will get the most leverage out of completing old stuff and clearing the decks (Part I). Other times a focus on the right focus is the primary key (Part II). Still other situations will call for structures and systems as most important for growth (Part III). And others will require simply letting go of trying to get it perfect and just get going (Part IV). All these aspects are important, but often one specifically will be the trigger point for busting through into a next level of productivity. Part V offers checklists as reference and reminders of the core practices for staying on top of the flow.

You will notice that the essays are not precise expositions of the principles they follow but rather food-for-thought spins on the topics.* And the concluding "By the way . . ." questions are merely

---

*These principles are numbered sequentially for this book, not as they were in the newsletters (the initial numberings were arbitrary, as well). Also, some essays have been paired with different principles than those they were matched with originally.

catalysts for your own reflection about possible applications "back at the ranch." Human behavior and awareness can be at the same time really simple, really complex, and infinitely explorable, and I've tried not to nail down anything too hard. But you'll find at least hints as to how work functions at higher levels, how we function, and how the world functions. As you digest and put these principles into practice, there is a good chance you will contribute more to your job and to your life as a whole. Reading them will likely reinforce subtle changes in your perceptions, which lead to changes in behavior. A change in behavior leads to a change in action *and* in results. Things spiral outward in larger and larger ways. Change occurs, and a positive shift happens. It's most often the small things, done consistently in strategic places, that make the most difference.

As I said, you probably don't need to work harder. You also may not feel you have to institute the step-by-step system with all the parts and processes that *Getting Things Done* provided. But at times you still may need to manage incompletions better, be more creative and expansive, be more focused in your thinking, access your intuition, have better structures, be more flexible and relaxed, or just get moving on next steps. Any or all of the above will make you more productive. This book provides important perspectives in all of those areas and may have just the key you need to kickstart yourself into rewarding new levels of expression.

You will probably find something familiar about this material. Not that you've read it anywhere else, but that you will recognize it as something you already know, intuitively. To gain value from this content does not require new skills or learning a complex body of new information. This writing will likely validate much of what you already know and do that works. But it will also challenge you to apply that awareness in a much more conscious and consistent manner—and that's where the real power lies. This is a compilation of effective perspectives and behaviors, applicable anywhere, anytime. Though each has merit by itself, as a whole they will provide a rich contextual experience greater than the sum of its parts.

Whether you approach it ad hoc or straight through, I invite you to allow the bigger picture of a dynamic, positive readiness for life to emerge as you turn the pages.

I continue to be surprised with the seemingly infinite ways the principles of personal effectiveness can be examined and experienced. Our journeys always return to the same basic truths, but our explorations lead us back to those awarenesses in new and more profound ways. The thinking captured in this book will no doubt open more doorways and lead to further discoveries. One layer of meaning will give way to another and then another and another. The spiral will continue to expand. It's as interesting and inspiring to me to think about what's not yet in this book as of what is. I hope you will find it, as I have, a doorway instead of a final act.

The "ready state" of the martial artist is not a passive, reactive, or finite one. It is totally dynamic, alive, creative, and expansive. But it's not free. It is enabled by increasingly refined training and experience with work and life. May these principles serve as road signs and guideposts along your way.

PART I

CLEAR YOUR HEAD FOR CREATIVITY

or

Getting the Loose Ends to Leave You Alone

It's crazy. We don't have time to get our work done, because of all the work we have to do. And we'd be so much better at the details if we just didn't have them to deal with. Mosquitoes can ruin the hunt for big game. There is light at the end of this tunnel, but the way out is through. Sometimes the biggest gain in productive energy will come from cleaning the cobwebs, dealing with old business, and clearing the decks—cutting loose debris that's impeding forward motion.

1.

Cleaning up creates
new directions.

Completion of open loops, whether they be major projects or boxes of old stuff we've yet to purge and organize, prepares the ground for cleaner, clearer, and more complete energy for whatever shows up. We're often not sure what's next or what to tackle. At that point, just clean or complete something—something obvious and in front of you, right away. Soon you'll have the energy and clarity to know what's next, and you'll have cleared the decks for more effective responsiveness on every front. Process your in-basket, purge your e-mails, or clean your center desk drawer. You've got to do it sometime anyway.

Prepared for the Unknown?

SOMETHING IS COMING—probably within a few days—that's going to change your world. You don't see it yet. You don't know what it's about. But it's there, rolling inexorably forward, destined to throw you a curve that you do not expect. It could show up sooner or later—but it *will* show up. Trust me.

Write down these words exactly four weeks from today on your calendar: "David Allen said a month ago that something was coming I couldn't foresee that would affect me significantly." Prove me wrong.

Are you ready? Is that unexpected event or input going to add insult to injury by making you feel more out of control? Or are you going to see it as the next creative opportunity that takes you to a new level of expression and contribution? How are you preparing for the surprises that the new experience will invariably throw your way?

I think there are basically two levels to handle for any unforeseen opportunity:

1. The spiritual. If God is all, and you're part of that, just relax.
2. All the rest. For this you must get your act together, so you can shift gears as required.

An old Asian proverb says, "The more you sweat in peace, the less you bleed in war." The military model is not a bad one—in the armed forces, if you're not fighting, you're training. Most people get ready for change a few days before a long vacation, when they divorce and have to sell everything they own and move, or when some other major life event causes them to rethink it all and get some clarity around their commitments and their "stuff." They're cleaning up, closing up, and renegotiating all their agreements with themselves and others.

All intellectual improvement arises from leisure.
—SAMUEL JOHNSON

It is the act of forgiveness that opens up the only possible way to think creatively about the future at all.
—FATHER DESMOND WILSON

I suggest you do that weekly. And get yourself organized enough so that when a staff meeting is late to start, you're processing your in-basket or cranking down your FYI-to-read stack. Or when you're waiting for your spouse to get ready (like, *actually* ready), you're checking to see if there's a phone call you could make. I know very few people on the planet who care enough about their time and what they're doing, every minute, to maximize those kinds of windows. If you weren't taking advantage of your time that way, I'd ask yourself, Why not?

When's the last time you updated your projects list (those things that take more than one action to complete) and brought it current, with next actions for each one placed in your system? The degree to which you haven't done that is the degree to which you are enduring unnecessary stress.

And if you don't have one yet, get a ubiquitous idea-capturing tool. Something to write or record things on, whenever they occur to you. You need something that's always with you—on the beach, in the health club, at your desk, out for dinner. It's very helpful if you can tie it in with your wallet or purse, which is already in that category for you. The older, wiser, and more sophisticated you get, personally and professionally, the more your best ideas about something happen somewhere they can't be implemented at that moment.

You might understand intellectually that you should get everything out of your head that has potential future value or represents potential agreements with yourself and others. But you have to put that into practice by writing it down when it pops in. If you are getting any "thing to do" out of reading this, where are you recording that? Pocket notebooks, three-by-five cards, miniature recorders—whatever.

Get your ubiquitous capture tool in place and functioning as a standard life accessory. Going somewhere without it should feel as weird as going out without shoes on. It'll take you to a whole new level of creative thinking and doing.

When you know everything, you are like a dark sky. Sometimes a flashing will come through the dark sky. After it passes, you forget all about it, and there is nothing left but the dark sky. The key is never being surprised when all of a sudden a thunderbolt breaks through. And when the lightning does flash, a wonderful sight may be seen. When we have emptiness, we are always prepared for watching the flashing.

—SHUNRYU SUZUKI

By the way . . .
○ Where are your potential cleanup areas?
○ What's the next one to tackle, when you're not sure what else to be doing?
○ What could you forgive today?

2.

You can only feel good about what you're not doing when you know what you're not doing.

Stress comes from unkept agreements with yourself. You can relieve that stress only by canceling the agreement, keeping the agreement, or renegotiating it. But you can't renegotiate agreements with yourself that you forgot you made. Because psychic RAM has no sense of past or future, things filed there push on you to be done all the time. They must be made conscious, and kept so, to alleviate the pressure.

Why "Getting Organized" Usually Hasn't Worked

THE OTHER DAY I had another BFO: a Blinding Flash of the Obvious. Many people are allergic to "getting organized" because they've experienced a consistent lack of success with using to-do lists. Those lists haven't worked because they were an attempt to compress very different and discrete functions into one event and context. If you try to make something too simple, it will make everything seem more complex and difficult. Yes, we've all been up against the wall of too many things screaming at us in our head, and we've gotten temporary relief by "making a list." But these Band-Aids don't work as an ongoing strategy.

Get a purge for your brain. It will do better than for your stomach.

—MICHEL EYQUEM DE MONTAIGNE

When most people sit down to write a list, they're actually trying to combine all five of the phases we've defined for mastering workflow: collect, process, organize, review, and do. They are simultaneously attempting to grab things out of their mind, decide what they mean, arrange them in some logical or meaningful fashion, jump immediately to an evaluation of each against each other, and then chose the "most important" thing to do. People who do this are usually rewarded with a short-term payoff of confusion relieved, but they're left with a gnawing vulnerability to what's uncaptured, unprocessed, unorganized, unseen, and underestimated.

Over many years of research and coaching, we've discovered that these phased aspects of workflow management are best done as separate activities. You need to collect everything that's on your mind first, little or big. Then you need to as-

> *Everything should be made as simple as possible, but not simpler.*
> —ALBERT EINSTEIN

sess each individual particle of that inventory and ask, "Is it actionable?" If so, what's the outcome? What's the next action? You then need to organize all the results of that thinking into appropriate categories. At that point, you can clearly review all your options of what to do and make the best choices, given all the criteria for reaching those decisions (time, energy, context, priorities, etc.).

Managing yourself is simple, but not simplistic.

Take five minutes, find something you can write fast with, and dump everything that pops into your head. Don't analyze or organize. Later on, you can figure out what, if anything, it means. For now, just dump. Give yourself the freedom to do one thing at a time. Be creative, be a visionary, express yourself, capture it all, without feeling a responsibility to actually *do* anything about it! Then, when you're ready to be an executive, come back to each one of those things and make decisions about what they all mean and what you're going to commit to and do about them, if anything. Then, later, you can show up as a manager and make tactical decisions about which thing to do out of all your options that fit the time and place. Each of these is a big job, requiring unique energies and perspectives. Don't get them confused.

By the way . . .

○ When did you last do a complete core dump out of your head?

○ Do you have any to-dos you're avoiding looking at?

○ If you didn't need to worry about things you haven't done, how would you be?

3.

Knowing your commitments creates better choices of new ones.

If you don't know the total current inventory of your work, you won't be fully aware of what you can't do. Your integrity will lead you into an infinite amount of new to-dos. When you consciously track all your commitments, that same integrity will force you to discriminate and say no, because you'll be more aware of your capabilities. For instance, if you've put things to read in various locations, you'll have trouble getting through any of them. Put them all in one place, and you'll handle many with a two-minute glance.

When the Center Is the Edge

A PERENNIAL TOPIC arises in my world of training people in the martial art of work: Where is the ideal point between freedom and structure? When is organized too organized, controlled too controlling, or construction constriction? On the other hand, when does looseness lose, open-endedness exhaust, or carefree become careless?

Fortunate, indeed, is the man who takes exactly the right measure of himself and holds a just balance between what he can acquire and what he can use.

—PETER MERE LATHAM

We're conditioned to think that boundaries limit us—"Don't fence me in." But we're also taught that to get something done, we need to exert pressure and push hard to achieve a result—"Put our nose to the grindstone." What's the best approach?

We must avoid here two complementary errors: on the one hand that the world has a unique, intrinsic, preexisting structure awaiting our grasp; and on the other hand that the world is in utter chaos. The first error is that of the student who marveled at how the astronomers could find out the true names of distant constellations. The second error is that of Lewis Carroll's Walrus, who grouped shoes with ships and sealing wax, and cabbages with kings.

—REUBEN ABEL

This is not merely a theoretical or philosophical discussion. When daily you receive four hundred e-mails, a hundred voice mails, and fifty unexpected interruptions, you must confront the freedom-versus-structure issue. The freedom junkies are frustrated and disturbed that these inputs are there to begin with and would love to just ignore them (except for the fun, easy, interesting, and really "hot" ones). The control freaks have rules, agents, and folders within folders within folders for every little detail, perhaps limiting the scope of their life out of fear of all the stuff a broader focus might generate.

Everyone can relate to both sides. We want to have control but not be constrained. The problem has come from the negative connotation (and actual experience) that often accompanies the idea of "control"—that it *is* constraining and constrictive, like being kept in jail. There is a way to reap the benefits of both sides. It's playing the game with two basic moves—concentration and cooperation.

Those two linked together give us the freedom we want and the structure we need to maximize our effectiveness. Concentration is the key to power, in physics and in life, and cooperation is the lubricant for the efficient flow of that energy. Top athletes demonstrate this wonderfully. They're megafocused and pay extraordinary attention to the realities of their environment and how to flow within them to their advantage.

To get through your e-mail, you must concentrate. What are you doing, and how is each communication relevant to that? And you must cooperate. The e-mails are there—you've created or at least allowed them, and you must create a strategy and a process for dealing with them. One approach serves the other. You must cooperate with yourself and your world in order to transcend resistance and distraction, so you can concentrate. And you must concentrate to clarify the nature of things and how to engage with them cooperatively.

Elegantly dealing with the stuff of life and work demands a rigorous focus on what you're doing and a high level of awareness and acceptance of all the details of your world. It might sound easy, yet it's quite a feat to be able to stay conscious about what you're doing, know where you're going, identify all the things you've committed to, and cooperate with what's not happening—so you can totally concentrate on what is.

> *Besides the noble art of getting things done, there is the noble art of leaving things undone. The wisdom of life consists in the elimination of nonessentials.*
>
> —LIN YUTANG

By the way . . .

○ What would you really like to be free of? What discipline is needed where, to accomplish that?

○ Where could you use more looseness?

○ Where could you use more structure?

4.

Getting to where you're going requires knowing where you are.

A map is not functional until you know where you are on it. Locating yourself in space and time provides a reference for motion: how much is required and in what direction. Objectively viewing your current reality always reduces confusion and misalignment. Agreement with yourself and others about what's true right now—in your company, on your project, in your life—is critical for making clear headway.

Forget the Future—Just Get a Grip

THERE'S AN OLD SAYING from the personal-growth movement: "What you resist, you're stuck with." Lately I've been noticing how true this is for many people and their work. If you're not clear what your current job really is and you avoid doing a complete and objective inventory, you're going to have a hard time making your work different or better.

Real generosity toward the future consists in giving all to what is present.
—ALBERT CAMUS

I'm often asked, "How do I set priorities?" My question back is always the same: "What's your job?" In order to know what activities are more important than others, you must have a reference point for what you want to maintain, accomplish, or experience—you must know what your work is. But what is the total reality of your "job" right now? That's seldom as obvious as most people would like to think.

You answer that question by answering six other ones. From the bottom up:

1. What are your current tasks? These are the physical actions you need to take right now about all your commitments and responsibilities: phone calls, e-mails, conversations, errands, brainstorming ideas, and so on. Typically a person on any day will have between a hundred and two hundred of these to do.

2. What are your current projects? These are the outcomes you have agreed with yourself to achieve, requiring more than one action to complete them, such as putting new tires on your car, getting your kids into summer camp, and buying a company. Most people have between thirty and a hundred of these.

3. What are your current areas of responsibility? Most people have ten to fifteen, including the main areas of a job (staff development, asset management, planning, customer service, etc.) and the key categories of the business of life (finances, health, family, household, career, recreation, etc.).

4. How are your job and personal affairs going to be changing in the next year? These are the objectives one is committed to fulfill or maintain over the next months—goals, intentions for change, large projects, and so on.

5. How are your organization, your career, and your personal life going to change? These are the bigger pictures—the vision of how things should be over the next few years.

6. Why are you on the planet? This is your purpose for being— your "job" as a human being.

If you complete a thorough inventory of the commitments, issues, and projects that currently exist for you on all six of these levels, you will have a good definition of your work. Yet I know very few people who are close to having these all completely identified, in current time.

It takes about ten years to get used to how old you are.
—UNKNOWN

I've often spent ten to fifteen hours with a person just identifying his or her work on the two most mundane and operational levels: current actions and projects. Without objectifying that inventory to clear the psychological decks at those levels, people are seldom ready to have a conversation with their boss or business partner or spouse about recalibrating their job description or dealing with needed changes in a relationship. Those who haven't addressed the basic questions about what they are doing, now, at their most functional levels, are usually resistant to thinking seriously about what needs to change to come into alignment with the shifts that are invariably going on in their companies, in the world, and in their lives.

Discipline does not mean suppression and control, nor is it adjustment to a pattern or ideology. It means the mind sees "what is" and learns from "what is."

—J. KRISHNAMURTI

Many people have a vague sense that they want to do or be something in the future—something different. But without a reality-based reference point of where they in fact *are* on all levels of life, they're like the Flying Dutchman, doomed to drift. But clarifying and managing what's in front of you to deal with right now, with even a small degree of completion, will open up natural inspiration and creativity for what's to come—without any further effort on your part.

Without knowing where you are on the map, you won't know whether to turn left or right going out the door, no matter how clear your goal. It's a real challenge to acknowledge consciously the total inventory of what you've created in your work and life. But the acceptance of what's true will change it—in quantum positive ways.

By the way . . .

○ What's true for you right now? Would it be useful to bring others in your life and work up to date with any of that right now?

○ With anything you consider a problem at the moment, what's the actual data that causes you to think it's a problem? Can you see the information another way?

5.

Infinite opportunity is utilized by finite possibility.

Trying to do it all, have it all, and be it all will exhaust the human mechanism. "More and better" will always stretch out in front of you, as you attain it. To surf on top of the game instead of drowning, infinite "everything you could ever want" must be corralled into doable, physical chunks. Expansive expressiveness requires intelligence and conscious limitation to be sustainable.

The One-Minute Workflow Manager

I'VE GIVEN NUMEROUS "drive-by" radio and TV interviews, the type that give you about fifty-three seconds to deliver the keys to health, wealth, and happiness. They've forced me to distill my message to the bare essentials. A typical question is, "David, what's the one thing we do that gets in the way of being productive?" Here's my answer:

"It's not one thing but five things all wrapped together: People keep stuff in their head. They don't decide what they need to do about stuff they know they need to do something about. They don't organize action reminders and support materials in functional categories. They don't maintain and review a complete and objective inventory of their commitments. Then they waste

> *It's possible to own too much. A man with one watch knows what time it is; a man with two watches is never quite sure.*
>
> —LEE SEGALL

energy and burn out, allowing their busyness to be driven by what's latest and loudest, hoping it's the right thing to do but never feeling the relief that it is."

How'd I do?

If not controlled, work will flow to the competent man until he submerges.

—CHARLES BOYLE

When life demands more of people than they demand of life—as is ordinarily the case—what results is a resentment of life almost as deep-seated as the fear of death.

—TOM ROBBINS

I merely bottom-lined the worst practices for the five stages of managing workflow: collect, process, organize, review, and do. I can't give an interviewer any one of these as *the* problem. You could do four of these workflow steps really well, but let one slip and the whole thing slips with it. The process is only as good as the weakest link in that chain.

Most people keep stuff only in their head, which short-circuits the process to begin with. Plenty of people write lots of things down, but they don't decide the next actions on them. And even when people actually think about the actions required (before it's in crisis mode), they don't organize the reminders so that they'll be seen when they are in the contexts where the action is possible. And even most of those people who *do* get these lists together in a burst of inspired productivity let their systems quickly become out of date and inconsistent. As a consequence, without the care and feeding of their thinking tools, life and work become reactive responses instead of clearly directed action choices.

"So, David, what do we need to do instead?" (Some interviewers actually allow another fifty-three seconds for this follow-up question!)

"It's a combined set of the five best-practice behaviors," I tell them. "Get everything out of your head. Make decisions about actions required on stuff when it shows up—not when it blows up. Organize reminders of your projects and the next actions on them in appropriate categories. Keep your system current, complete, and reviewed sufficiently to trust your intuitive choices about what you're doing (and not doing) at any time."

I suppose I could have made it even simpler: "Focus on positive outcomes and continually take the next action on the most important thing." But who doesn't know that? Consistent implementation of that principle, fully integrating every aspect of our life, is the biggest challenge—and not so simple.

By the way . . .

○ Have you lately gone over your checklist of your job description (four to seven key areas of focus and responsibility)?

○ Have you reviewed the five to ten areas of focus in your personal life (health, finances, career, relationships, etc.) to ensure that you have all the needed projects defined and keep all those intact and up to standard?

6.

Two commitments in your head create stress and failure.

You are subliminally aware of all your commitments, big and little, personal and professional, and they are stored in "psychic RAM" unless consciously and objectively tracked and reviewed. That part of the psyche, though, has no sense of past or future, so as soon as it is required to hold on to two incompletions, it creates inner frustration and anxiety. A creative part of you is attempting to do them both at once, which is impossible. But it doesn't give up. It keeps on trying and trying and trying. . . .

Getting Things Done: Reactive or Responsive?

SOMEONE RECENTLY COMMENTED that my "Getting Things Done" methodology is more "reactive" than other programs that have an initial emphasis on priorities and the "big picture." It's an understandable criticism. In much of our work, the first focus is at the level of the papers on your desk, the psychic Post-its ("should's" and "need-to's") in your brain, and the thousand e-mails clogging your computer. We don't start out concentrating on why you have these things stacked up or how to arrange them in order of importance. Yet there is method to our madness.

Spending time and energy on all the loose ends around you could be considered a reactive approach. But is it really? You've let these inputs into your world, physically and psychologically, and your reaction to them (or lack of it) is directly affecting your energy and ability to stay in command of all your psychic resources. Our process (gently) forces you to react to them.

What are they? What is your commitment to them? What is the next action required to fulfill that commitment? What do you need to think about and organize in order to dispatch each item appropriately?

Taking on new projects is not necessarily a positive change. It may be a sign of recklessness and non-fulfillment. But going back to all the levels of non-completion and completing them is a sign of positive change.

—JOHN-ROGER

Shouldn't we start with the priority-driving stuff: goals, values, purposes, and strategic objectives? Wouldn't it be better to be more proactive, creative, and forward thinking instead of focusing on the details of the past?

Sure. But one big reason we don't usually start that way is that it's almost impossible to focus on the bigger picture when a vast majority of your subliminal energy is wrapped around psychic "open loops" in your world. In order to most easily and effectively turn on and access the creative flow needed for new reality thinking, psychic RAM must be freed up.

There's another equally important reason we do a lot of hands-on work with people processing these kinds of details: We are training a powerful, productive, and proactively responsive behavior. Many people who profess to being driven by only the "most important things" deal with them after they've risen to the level of urgency or immediacy. Ignoring the not-yet-in-crisis but still-necessary commitments is in reality more "reactive" than responsive. If you think that the minutiae around you will automatically disappear when you have a clear, new, positive direction, think again. You must now dispatch all those details according to your new perspective. Dump them, file them, do them, delegate them, move on them, or park them for action at a more appropriate time.

Learning to respond effectively and efficiently to *everything* that has hooked your attention is masterful behavior. You will always have priorities, and they will grow and change as you mature. They will perhaps make it easier to decide which magazines you really want to read or which e-mail is the first to spend time on. But the ability to process clearly and cleanly, and to dispatch whatever shows up, does not automatically emerge from merely having those priorities.

If you know the point of balance, you can settle the details. If you can settle the details, you can stop running around. Your mind will become calm. If your mind becomes calm, you can think in front of a tiger. If you can think in front of a tiger, you will surely succeed.

—MENCIUS

Even when you recognize and commit to a goal or a vision, you still must "react" to it, for its expression and fulfillment. Response-ability is just that. As you sensitize and train yourself to assess and dispatch *anything* appropriately, you increase your maturity to do that with ever loftier outcomes.

Sure, we'll lead you through all the conversations that are necessary to align yourself, your projects, your job description, your key areas of focus, your short-term objectives, your long-term visions, and your ultimate reason for being. But we'd rather do that after you've finished processing all the current details of your life and work and have gained the discipline to do that with everything from now on. If you haven't mastered the random paper on your desk or the e-mails in your computer, you're still missing a key component to manifesting anything.

By the way . . .

○ What's still just in your head that keeps popping up to remind you about your agreement with yourself to make something different?

○ What have you avoided dealing with today? Why do you think it won't still be there tomorrow? How useful would it be to get it off your mind right now?

7.

Priorities function only at the conscious level.

All of your actions and projects have relative importance to you but only when they're consciously weighed against each other. If something is filed away in your memory (psychic RAM), it will use inappropriate, unproductive thinking space, and will probably be over- or undervalued. Maintaining a complete, current, and reviewable inventory of all the open loops, no matter how big or small they are, is a prerequisite for setting trustworthy priorities.

The Danger of "Not as Important" Projects

TOO MANY personal-productivity disasters these days come from a lack of handling things of "secondary" importance. Do you ever get the sense that you don't have time to deal with the secondary things, because you have to deal with so many consistently demanding fires and crises? Well, guess where most of those fires and crises come from? Correct—from secondary things that were ignored because of all the fires and crises. This syndrome does not self-correct— it self-perpetuates.

> *There is nothing so easy but that it becomes difficult when you do it reluctantly.*
> —TERENCE

I attribute part of that to the ABC priority-code thinking that has recently been so prevalent in time-management and priority-management training. I understand teaching people that if they have a choice about what to do with their time, some choices create better results than do others. But the dark side to this principle is avoiding responsibility for managing many open loops that don't go away, just because they aren't an A priority.

What lies in our power to do, it lies in our power not to do.
—ARISTOTLE

People in my seminars often comment on why I recommend that they make a complete projects list, with no distinctions about priorities, time frame, or size. The distinction I do recommend is very simple: projects versus someday / maybe. The first list is a complete inventory of all the open loops we've created that require more than one action to close them. Most people have thirty to a hundred of those. The second list is all those projects that you might want to do sometime in the future but have no commitment to move on them right now.

Lots of folks confuse bad management with destiny.
—KIN HUBBARD

If it's on the projects list, you need to decide next actions equally on each one and review the status of each regularly. It's okay not to take action on them, as long as you know what the action is and as long as it's a conscious choice. But most people avoid involvement because they don't stop to think what the action is and then miss countless opportunities to move it forward before it morphs into crisis.

Either you need new tires or you don't. At some point, the tire thing crosses a very distinct line. Before then, not needed. After then, needed. Once they're needed, there are no ABC categories for tires. They also don't quite fit into the "quadrant" matrix. Either they are a project to be done as soon as we can or they are not. Period.

It's true that once projects have crossed that line, there is a gradient from merely "needed" to "desperately needed." And all too often, because people have not responsibly dealt with them when they were merely "needed," "desperately needed" finally gets their attention. Instead of a next action, like "Call tire store for prices," it becomes a next action, like "Call Auto Club to repair blowout."

Clarify and define *all* the outcomes you've committed yourself to accomplish, small and large, and the actions required to move on them. Then you're ready for the real efficiency game of getting them *all* done, as soon as you can, and feeling okay about how it's going with each one.

Customer-service departments do not pretend to have the luxury of ignoring *any* request or open loop. If you really want to be of service to yourself, you don't either.

By the way . . .

○ What have you decided to ignore because it doesn't seem that important right now?

○ How important would it be if it were already accomplished?

○ How would you feel once it was done?

8.

Closing open loops releases energy.

No matter how unimportant they seem or how unconscious we are about them, unfulfilled commitments consume psychic fuel that is unavailable for other uses. When these unfinished items are brought to the surface and completed (or acknowledged as complete, as is), previously inaccessible energy shows up.

The Magical Mundane

Finish each day and be done with it. You have done what you could. Some blunders and absurdities no doubt crept in; forget them as soon as you can. Tomorrow is a new day; begin it well and serenely and with too high a spirit to be encumbered with your old nonsense.

—RALPH WALDO EMERSON

ONE OF THE MOST effective ways to spark a dynamic vision is to clean your garage. Don't get me wrong. Writing a great strategic plan and creating a clean, well-ordered garage are very different activities. One requires a high-level focus and a willingness to see beyond the conditioning and details of current reality. The other requires an often brutal hand-to-hand combat with those details. Yet there is a strange and wondrous relationship between the two.

You can have the greatest strategic plan in the world about what you intend to do with your garage. But come Saturday, when you finally gird your loins, don your grubby jeans, roll up your sleeves, and get *into* it, your previous vision may be obsolete within the hour. Your dream moved you to get moving, but the inspirational juices uncorked as you fully engaged in something so personally creative and real will open you to possibilities never before imagined.

Perhaps it's because you will stir warm and creative questions about your life (When did you take that picture? Remember collecting those rocks?). Perhaps it's the intentional act of taking responsibility for something you produced and attached to yourself, which automatically triggers executive consciousness. Perhaps it's the natural high that appears when you clean up and close up old, stale energy fields. What you wind up with will very likely look and feel quite different from what you initially thought you were going to create. And it'll be a lot better.

That's why I maintain a healthy skepticism when people want to get control of their work and life by "setting priorities." This is often just an attempt to sidestep responsibility for what they've been engaged with irresponsibly. My choice is always to go for cleaning up the garage of their work, their life, and their head. Then the priorities, the vision, and the plan emerge—grounded, with solid roots. And they are seldom exactly what people think they will be. The mundane is not a substitute for the sublime. It's just a secret passageway to it.

For a long time it had seemed to me that life was about to begin—real life. But there was always some obstacle in the way. Something to be got through first, some unfinished business, time still to be served, a debt to be paid. Then life would begin. At last it dawned on me that these obstacles were my life.
—FATHER ALFRED D'SOUZA

Opportunity is missed by most people because it is dressed in overalls and looks like work.
—THOMAS EDISON

By the way . . .
○ **When have you had inspiration blossom from a mundane activity?**
○ **What open loop around you needs you to "dig in," physically? Can you imagine what awaits you on the other side?**

9.

If it's on your mind,
it's probably not getting done.

Something will "bug" you until you've clarified your intention about it (outcome), decided how to move on it (next action), and put reminders of the outcome and action in places your mind trusts that you'll see as often as you need to and at the right time. Those are also the behaviors that ensure things get done—defining what "done" means, deciding what "doing" looks like, and installing the results of that thinking into a structure that most easily promotes implementation.

The ABCs of Psychic RAM

AFTER I RECENTLY gave a presentation, an executive approached me with a stunned look and said, "I think you may have just changed my life."

"How so?" I asked.

"Up until now," he replied, "I've actually prided myself on how much I could keep and manage in my head, and I even kept trying to expand it. I now realize that's probably been energy totally misplaced!"

> *The mind is not a vessel to be filled but a fire to be kindled.*
> —PLUTARCH

Time will tell.

Many years ago, I decided that either your head is the place to hold something or it's not. How can you intellectually justify halfway in between? And though most people, when they think about it, would say, "No, your head is probably not the best place to keep something in a trustworthy fashion," they still keep over half their life in there. A ton of woulds, coulds, shoulds, need-tos, ought-tos, and might-want-tos would be jammed into one place.

> *To be what we are, and to become what we are capable of becoming, is the only end in life.*
>
> —ROBERT LOUIS STEVENSON

Left only in the mind, these self-commitments create infinite loops that make no progress and produce inner conflict and stress. As soon as you make any sort of commitment with yourself, not completed in the moment, your mind will demand and take psychic energy until it's resolved. That is mental karma. "I need milk" and "I need to decide whether to buy this company" both tie up space in psychic RAM.

The solution is simple. Write it down. Look at it. Do it or say to yourself, "Not now." And trust that you'll see the option again whenever you need to reassess. Give it to a system superior to your mind, so your mental energy can move on to its bigger and better work.

This is a very big habit for adults to change. The best of the best we have coached, who really "catch" what this methodology is about, still sometimes take up to two years to fully implement our practices. When they first jump in, they immediately experience a huge boost in energy and relaxed control. But to get to the place where truly the only thing on their mind, aside from whatever they're doing in the moment, may be the last couple of unprocessed hours of their life—that's a significantly different level of expertise in application.

Kids can pick up on this pretty fast, though. And I have a vision that, twenty-five years from now, every twelve-year-old on the planet will say, "Why did you ever keep things in your head? What an old-fashioned and dumb thing to do!" They'll be using their energies to better advantage. Let's help get them there.

By the way . . .

○ What still-unfinished things are really *off* your mind? How did you accomplish that?

○ What's still on your mind, for which the bottleneck is in your head?

○ What else would you like to stop thinking about?

10.

Creativity shows up when there's space.

The universe abhors a vacuum—and electric current won't flow through a blocked pathway. When mental space has too many distractions and unmanaged agreements and loops, flow is limited. Clear the pipes and you attract and foster new, productive thinking that almost happens by itself.

Is This All There Is?

I'VE BEEN PREACHING for years the value of getting everything out of your head. And I've been curious why even the most enthusiastic clients and seminar participants often have such trouble installing this habit. Tens of thousands of people have understood and conceptually agreed with me about the nature of psychic RAM—that it has limited space, is a terrible office, and that things stored there will invariably be over- or underutilized. So why all the resistance to implementing this principle to the fullest?

Because deeper reasons are in play here, involving significant challenges to our comfort zones and self-image dynamics. Such as the fear that if we could actually see all of our creations in one place, it may not be enough. What if this really *is* all there is, and it's the

> *Our greatest pretenses are built up not to hide the evil and the ugly in us, but our emptiness. The hardest thing to hide is something that is not there.*
>
> —ERIC HOFFER

best I can *do,* and it's still not what I think it ought to *be?* That's a pervasive underlying angst for most people most of the time, if they really look deeply enough. And the last thing in the world we feel like doing is actually confronting that possibility.

In order to arrive at what you do not know/You must go by a way which is the way of ignorance.

—T. S. ELIOT

Keeping uncaptured, unclarified, and unprocessed things in our minds creates unnecessary stress. But if we leave them there, we can allow ourselves to believe that there's still plenty of potential merit and importance to our thinking lying around in our brains. If we write everything down that we have to do, along with all our constructive thoughts about it, we may see the limits of our capabilities. If we maintain confusion and amorphousness, we can pretend that we *could* be smart, powerful, and purposefully effective—but never have to prove it to ourselves. "Oh, I *could* express much more of my magnificence, creativity, brilliance, and dynamism, but because my importance has me so burdened with the responsibilities it must bear, I just can't demonstrate it at the moment." What crafty games we can play with ourselves!

I know you have nothing. That is why I ask you for everything. So that you will have everything.

—ANTONIO PORCHIA

A core principle in our personal-productivity methodology confronts this issue head-on: Write it *all* down, think about it *all,* decide what needs to be done about it *all,* and manage the options of it *all* in a consistently reviewed external system. The "all" factor can be awesomely revealing.

The wonderful surprise is that for everyone who actually risks it—actually *does* get it all out in front of him- or herself—the resulting experience is far from intimidating. It is liberating. It creates an unmistakable release of pressure and a surge of self-esteem, because such people are now operating from the *source* of their creativity, not from its effect.

One of the greatest challenges we must face at some point in our lives is that our sense of self-worth cannot hang solely on our inventory of what we've created. If all we'd done were to disappear—at this moment—we have to know that we will continue to have value and that we can create from scratch what we need or want. We have to know that no matter how finished we think we are, God isn't done with us until she is.

By the way . . .

○ Two decades ago, could you have imagined all that you've experienced and accomplished since then?

○ Do you think that stream of still-unknown successes is going to slow down for you?

○ Are you ready for a bigger parade?

11.

The deeper the channel, the greater the flow.

Cleaning up and streamlining the systems of life and work increase our ability to handle greater engagement with the world and consequently galvanize unseen forces to fill the channels. Increased capacity seems to unlock attractive energy that starts to permeate the organism or enterprise. It invites participation from the world, at a deep and creative level. Conversely, unresolved issues and vulnerable systems will protect themselves by automatically and unconsciously stifling new input.

Are You Really Ready for More?

WE RECENTLY RAISED some prices—because I didn't want business to go away. Let me explain. One day, I recognized a subtle internal danger signal: There was the tiniest bit of an "uh-oh" feeling inside me each time we were asked to do more and more of a certain kind of work for a favorite client. It was almost imperceptible, but it was there: I didn't want the phone to ring. After many years of watching this dynamic, I knew that if I allowed those feelings to persist, indeed, the phone would stop ringing. This client would go away. I'm that powerful, and so are you.

I confronted the feeling and discovered the root of the problem: We were underpriced for the amount of time and attention

Before everything else, getting ready is the key to success.
—HENRY FORD

we had to commit to do our standard quality work. I had to challenge myself with this question: "What do I need to do to make me positively excited about the phone's ringing again?" The answer was simple: Raise the price. Then I could feel good about dedicating the time and energy we do to this client—and the more time, the merrier.

That may seem self-evident to you, but it wasn't to me, until it was done. We have high standards about delivering beyond expectations, and pricing has always been a sensitive issue. But sometimes I have to get out of my comfort zone to stay motivated to do excellent work over the long term.

If I keep a green bough in my heart, the singing bird will come.

—CHINESE PROVERB

A fundamental principle is at work here. All of us, personally and organizationally, may be unconsciously holding back new and better things from ourselves, because we feel that we won't be able to handle them successfully or sufficiently. Most of us think that we want "more" of many things. More money, more clients, more responsibility, more fun, more time. But do we really? I've learned that what I consciously want is only a fraction of what directs my creative energies. Many times what I think I've wanted has lost out to other forces. I've had many opportunities cross my path—for more money, clients, responsibility, fun, and personal fulfillment. But because some part of me wasn't really prepared to handle them (or what came with them), I didn't recognize them in the moment; and even if I did, I found subtle ways to push them away.

Years ago, a mentor of mine, who'd consulted with several health-care organizations, told me that whenever the front office of a clinic cleaned up its backlog of claims and paperwork and streamlined its workflow, patient volume invariably increased dramatically. He suggested that as long as the reception staff experienced new business as creating more stress (due to clogged systems), they would unconsciously turn it away. Many organizations are exhorting their people to be "customer driven" and to "go the extra mile" to add a competitive edge of extraordinary service that will win more business. But they may not be addressing the ability to handle that added business. Everyone can sense this on some level, and if their environment is already stressed to the max (as most are), that extra mile extra smile will not surface when it's

Millions long for immortality who do not know what to do with themselves on a rainy Sunday afternoon.

—SUSAN ERTZ

needed the most. When your front line feels overwhelmed, watch out for resistance to new customers and opportunities! When a ringing phone creates stress at the spinal level, though the words may be "Can I help you?" the underlying communication is, "Go away! I can't handle you!" Not the first message you want to give to the people who ultimately pay your rent and salary.

Do you feel free in your conversations with key people in your life and work to develop new ideas that might serve them more and better? If not, why not? Could it be that you don't feel you could deliver? Is that okay with you?

Are you set up on all areas of your work and your life for expansion or for contraction? The power of your inner intentions is limitless—whether negative or positive. Are you less than enthusiastically waiting for phone calls or for someone to knock at your door? How else will opportunities for more growth, greater expression, and abundance present themselves? If you're after more of those "golden goodies" of life, I suggest you take a risk. Do what you need to do to get back to eagerly anticipating the ringing of your bell.

By the way . . .

○ Bring to mind a time when new opportunities showed up for you. What had you been doing in the months previous that prepared you for them?

○ What system may be clogged, personally or organizationally, that may be preventing new business?

12.

Worry is a waste.

Thinking that analyzes situations and matures our perceptions takes time and energy, but it is productive. Avoiding thinking about what you should be thinking about—worrying without actually getting down to it—wastes time and drains energy.

Getting Thinking off Your Mind

AH, THE DELICIOUS EXPERIENCE of not thinking. Athletes in their "zone," ecstatic worshipers "in the spirit," moviegoers and novel readers engrossed in the story, gardeners pruning their trees, lovers talking into the night—the bliss of no time, no stress, no . . . *thinking*. But one can engage in thinking and be equally "present," as when playing chess, brainstorming a project, negotiating a deal, or writing an essay. The productive state in which time disappears is not really about not thinking. It's more like not thinking about thinking. But how do you achieve that state?

> *There is no expedient to which a man will not go to avoid the real labor of thinking.*
> —THOMAS EDISON

> *How do I know what I think, until I hear what I say?*
> —E. M. FORSTER

The most productive approach is to think as little as you can get by with but as much as you need to. How do you get today off your mind? Several times during the day, you probably need to reassess all the actions required to accomplish what you're committed to. At least weekly, a thorough review of all your projects and attendant actions is usually necessary. Every month or two, you probably need to think through the checklist of all the areas of responsibility of your life and work, to ensure that the right projects are in order. Yearly, it's a good idea to look out over the next twelve to eighteen months and formulate where you want to be by then. And every few years, you (and any partners) most likely need to rethink your vision about life and lifestyle.

The "Grand Think" is figuring out your purpose here on the planet. If you really come up with that one, once should be enough, although you'll probably want to check in with some regularity to jog your memory.

You'll truly get into productive mode when you've established regular reviews at all these levels, with the habit and commitments in place to revisit them at appropriate intervals. When you know that you are consistently doing some version of the "weekly review," you afford yourself the luxury of not having to think about all that stuff for another week. You get to be somewhat dumb and happy, in productive "doing" mode, for seven days. Why? Because you've already generated what you need in terms of clarified perspective and an inventory of your commitments.

And if you have a habit of that kind of weekly regrouping, you'll be trusting that you're going to think again, and nothing will be falling through too big a crack. If you don't do the weekly review, feeling that you should be thinking about something will constantly bother you. It will drain your time and your mind. If you're having trouble get-

> *Civilization advances by extending the number of important operations which we can perform without thinking about them. Operations of thought are like cavalry charges in a battle—they are strictly limited in number, they require fresh horses, and must only be made at decisive moments.*
>
> —ALFRED NORTH WHITEHEAD

> *Anyone who waits to be struck with a good idea has a long wait coming. If I have a deadline for a column or a television script, I sit down at the typewriter and damn well decide to have an idea.*
>
> —ANDY ROONEY

ting into your "zone," or getting to the "mind like water" state, ask yourself at what level you need to do some focused thinking, and then get it done. Finish the exercise. Then come on in—the water's fine.

By the way . . .
○ When do you feel most in your "zone"? How do you get there?
○ What project do you know you need to do more thinking about? What's the next action to get that to happen?

13.

You are not your work.

Uncaptured, unclarified, and therefore unmanaged things that you have agreed to do own a piece of you and give you no rest. Naming your stuff gives you power over it. The best and most productive way to do your work is to be its master, not its slave.

The Big Secret About My Lists

AS MANY OF YOU KNOW by now, I have quite a few lists and quite a few things on them. It's time to share with you a seriously big secret about my lists: Some of the best projects I've done were never on them!

> *Be steady and well ordered in your life so that you can be fierce and original in your work.*
>
> —GUSTAVE FLAUBERT

What?! Aren't lists supposed to be the way to Get Things Done? Have I been fooling you all along? Have I duped you into believing that getting things out of your head, processing them into outcomes and actions, and writing the results into objective categories for consistent review is *the* way to get all your stuff accomplished?

It may seem that's what I've been preaching. Indeed, those behaviors do get a *lot* of things done, because they help get projects unstuck by defining the "doing" and the "done" and parking the results in trusted places that trigger the actions. But many people miss the real reason for doing this. You don't make the lists of actions and projects just to get them all done and then do nothing else in your life. You process the things you have attention on so you can do what you really feel like doing. And really do it, with 100 percent of your focus and creative energy, with abandon.

To control attention means to control experience, and therefore the quality of life.

—MIHALY
CSIKSZENTMIHALYI

I just spent all morning pruning my large pine tree. It felt great. My creative juices were flowing, my aesthetics were sparking for just the right shapes and spatial relationships in that part of our yard. But it wasn't on a list. This morning it just seemed like the thing to do.

If I didn't have the lists I have, and if I hadn't done a thorough review of them within the last few days, I wouldn't have been able to trust that my inventory of "defined work" was complete and current this morning. And that it could wait. Without that conscious self-renegotiation process, there would be at least a slight gnawing sense of anxiety that there were shoulds lurking in the

When hungry, eat your rice; when tired, close your eyes. Fools may laugh at me, but wise men will know what I mean.

—LIN-CHI

shadows that could attack me at any moment! And what's the best (temporary) relief and (false) protection from the unseen and ugly shoulds? Get *busy*.

Without my lists, I would probably still have pruned my pine tree this morning—but for all the wrong reasons.

By the way . . .
○ What are some of the most creative, fun, and productive things you've done that weren't planned or on any list?
○ How valuable would it be to create a way to have more of those?

PART II

FOCUS PRODUCTIVELY

or

What's the Point of a Point of View?

The greatest power we have to affect our world is always at our fingertips: our ability to change how we see things. Getting something to happen quicker, better, and bigger is seldom dependent on greater physical effort—it's more than likely going to require a shift in vision. Often a focus on the focus is the key to unlock the next level of gain.

14.

For more clarity, look from a higher place.

Whenever thinking is murky, ambiguous, or off purpose, you must let go of the level you're focusing on and shift the horizon to another plane. If you're busy (action) and unclear, stop and review your plans. If you're planning (organization) and unclear, get to a whiteboard or blank piece of paper and do a mental core dump to get the ideas and information you may be missing. If you're trying to free-range or get outside the box (brainstorm) and unclear, drop back and revisit the image of what success would look like, for more specificity. If your picture (vision) is too ill formed, return to your purpose—why you're doing the thing at all. Clarity is never found within something unclear. You must loosen your conceptual grip, let go, and lift your sights.

The Play of the Day

WHEN THINGS GET TIGHT and tough, it's easy to get hung up in a negative loop of self-talk: "Oh, no! Things are tight and tough!" We bemoan our fate and pander to our disappointment. In fact, such times are always great opportunities to re-assess what we're really doing and to deepen our thinking and focus. Tough times can be good times as long as we know the game we are playing and decide the play we are making.

The business of life is to go forward.
—SAMUEL JOHNSON

The greatest weapon against stress is our ability to choose one thought over another.
—WILLIAM JAMES

Circumstances that seem the most out of our control and grief producing (a bear market, things other people do that create hardship for us, and other "accidents" of life) can catch us seriously off guard. Ever had the feeling that you just woke up on a soccer field, being run over by bigger, meaner, uglier, and faster players, and you haven't the vaguest idea what you're doing there? You find yourself beaten, bloody, and muddy—and things seem to be getting worse!

To get a grip, what must you do? First, you have to accept what the game is and know where your goal is. When you can see your target and identify with getting there, you quickly lose interest in how beaten, bloody, or muddy you are. Now you're into the challenge! But even if you know where you're headed, you will still feel paralyzed and at the mercy of forces larger than yourself, until you do one thing: determine the next move. Left or right—pass or run? At that moment the next action is what matters most. So, in order to achieve clarity and be fully and positively engaged in what you're doing, you must (1) know the goal or outcome you're intending and (2) decide and take the next physical move to propel you in that direction.

You just lost your job. What do you want to be true now in your career, and how do you get started to make it happen? You just had a major setback in your health. How do you want to be feeling about your situation, and what actions will bring you closer to that reality? When the world has shifted on you in whatever way, what would success *now* mean for you, and what activity will move you *now* in that direction? It's very easy to fall into the trap of thinking that the game shouldn't have changed and that the old rules still should apply. "I was just getting used to the way it was—who screwed up the playing field!?" Success in life may have more to do with how

> *We are coming to understand health not as the absence of disease, but rather as the process by which individuals maintain their sense of coherence (i.e., sense that life is comprehensible, manageable, and meaningful) and ability to function in the face of changes in themselves and their relationships with their environment.*
>
> —AARON ANTONOVSKY

> *One can stand still in a flowing stream, but not in the world of men.*
>
> —JAPANESE PROVERB

fast you can accept and get started on the new game than with how good you got at playing any of the old ones.

It's not what is going on in your world that's good or bad. The world just is what it is. What makes the difference is how you're engaged with it. As any performance race driver will tell you, coasting is the most dangerous behavior of all. You have to stay involved with the pedals. You have to get into the game you're in.

To fight a bull when you are not scared is nothing. And to not fight a bull when you are scared is nothing. But to fight a bull when you are scared is something.
—UNKNOWN

By the way . . .

○ What project could use some mental regrouping right now?

○ When did you last take an "executive break"? Is it time for another?

○ In what location and during what kind of activity do you automatically think from a higher altitude?

○ What new game in town do you find yourself in? What's the next play?

15.

You won't see how to do it until you see yourself doing it.

Your brain's pattern-recognition mechanism is triggered by the images you identify with and the focus you hold. You see the outcome first, and then you are unconsciously made conscious of information. Whether it's how to catch a ball, create a company, or care for your parents, the vision comes first. If you won't see yourself having or doing something until you see how to do it, you'll never recognize the methods, though they are all around you. Notice what you notice and how you make that happen.

Waking Up Again to Making It Up Again

I AM CONTINUALLY AMAZED at how often I forget about our astonishing ability to create what we want by what we envision. Outcome thinking and the willingness to visualize something's being true before it's physically present is a master skill that we all could probably develop to a much greater degree.

> *One comes to be of just such stuff as that on which the mind is set.*
>
> —THE UPANISHADS

> *Nothing happens unless there is first a dream.*
>
> —CARL SANDBURG

I just looked at a mind map I did ten years ago. It was about what I wanted my life to be like, if I could really have it the way I wanted it. In my apartment, with a set of colored pens, it took me a couple of hours to fill in the whole page, drawing little pictures and putting in words and phrases as I was moved to do so. The vision was a big one.

It included how I wanted to be working, what kind of freedom and resources I would have, what successes I would be achieving, and other various aspects of a desirable lifestyle—even what my inner life would be like.

I can't say that it's all come to pass, but when I looked at the drawing and then looked at my current life, I saw how all those images for years had sparked and supported my significant choices. Some of the pictures weren't very exact, in terms of what I achieved. I never really got to a proficient level of playing jazz flute, as I had drawn (though I did get pretty good at some classical pieces). I certainly haven't fulfilled the picture I drew of the planet encircled with heartfelt energy, connected through the small towns and communities of the world. But I now live in one of those small towns and have contributed to many people and organizations that are doing great work improving the world. But much of the little mural was quite exact about what has come to pass. Being able to communicate potentially valuable information anytime, anywhere, globally, through high-tech media, for instance. This was before I knew what e-mail newsletters were or that I would be using one.

An interesting thing to me was what *wasn't* on the mind map—my lovely wife, Kathryn, and our terrific home in Ojai that we have now. Frankly, at the time, I wasn't consciously looking for marriage and a country home. But, in fact, it *was* a very deep-seated desire and vision I'd had in my twenties (some of these things take a while to come around, I've discovered!).

My visions were pure fantasies when I had them. But I allowed myself to draw the blueprint, and the blanks have been filling in

Your automatic creative mechanism is teleological. That is, it operates in terms of goals and end results. Once you give it a definite goal to achieve, you can depend upon its automatic guidance system to take you to that goal much better than you ever could by conscious thought. You supply the goal by thinking in terms of end results. Your automatic mechanism then supplies the means whereby.
—MAXWELL MALTZ

If you limit your choices to what seems possible or reasonable, you disconnect yourself from what you truly want, and all that is left is a compromise.
—ROBERT FRITZ

like magic. Not that there haven't been rough spots—we all pay our dues, one way or another—but it's good to have created for myself more of the club that I want to belong to!

And I'm so thankful when I remember that I always can.

By the way . . .
○ What have you been noticing a lot lately? What might you have been focusing on internally to generate that data?
○ What are you not seeing yourself have, do, or be, until someone shows you how? How could you capture the desired image now?

16.

Working hard enough is impossible.

You can never get enough of what you don't really need. Though this profound personal-growth axiom usually refers to things like "others' approval" (you really need your own), it is equally applicable to productivity. Many people are trying but can never work hard enough, because working hard is not really what they need. They need to simply be doing, in a careful and concerned way, without care or concern. Haven't you noticed that working hard at the right thing is not hard work?

Is It Overtime All the Time?

WHILE RECENTLY COACHING a successful executive, I discovered another subtle but very real level of the "busy trap." You know the syndrome: "If I can just be doing *something* that feels as if I'm working with focus, I don't have to deal with the angst about all the other stuff I probably should be doing."

> If it moves, salute it. If it doesn't move, pick it up. If you can't pick it up, paint it.
>
> —U.S. MILITARY

He had about a dozen e-mails left in his in-basket area, after processing hundreds the night before. But he'd already set up a category of actionable e-mails (that required a longer-than-two-minute response) in another place. I wanted him to stop using "in" for a holding bin and taste what it was like to get it totally empty, so I nudged him to go ahead and move those last e-mails out of "in" and over into where he had stored the others.

As he did that, you could see the light dawn: "Wow! Now I see my total work inventory in one place! And I realize that I would have let myself spend time on those e-mails before anything else, because that would seem the easiest choice to make. Now I can assess them immediately within the context of everything else I have to do. They're not lost, and they're in proper perspective. I've been letting myself get sucked into the busyness of it, instead of feeling better about making better choices."

We tend to recall items stored in our mind based on criteria of latest (most recent in time) and loudest (emotionally), which is hardly the most effective file-retrieval system. Similarly, if your system of action reminders is haphazard (Post-its on the screen, phone slips on the desk, notes on your chair), your busy energy momentum will latch on to the easiest thing to wrap itself around. But in-your-face proximity is not the best criterion for in-the-moment choices of what to do.

There's an extra payoff to clearing out psychic RAM, seeing your entire work inventory in one location, and making better choices about what to do next: When you can really choose the work to work on, it's a lot easier to choose not to work at all!

> *It is not enough to be busy. . . . The question is: What are we busy about?*
> —HENRY DAVID THOREAU

> *If you don't know what you're doing, you don't know when to stop.*
> —UNKNOWN

> *If you find yourself in a hole, the first thing to do is stop digging.*
> —WILL ROGERS

By the way . . .

○ What are you doing right now that you are interpreting as "hard work"? Does it seem that way when you're doing it or when you're *not* doing it?

○ When have you worked hard but didn't care? What could you learn from yourself about how to create that experience when you want to?

17.

Energy follows thought.

Putting your mind to something activates both the subject and the object of your thinking. The body neurologically begins to respond as if the thought is true, and ideas start living a life of their own. Thoughts can occur a second time much easier than the first. Merely having thoughts is one thing. Consciously feeding them is quite another. You are powerful all the time, by way of your attention and intention. The question is, Toward what are you pointing that power?

What Are You Putting in Front of Your Door?

WHEN IT COMES to focusing, I need all the help I can get. I think I want to improve, grow, and create results, but I lack the mental discipline of a yogi and the brilliant single-mindedness of a savant. I confess: I'm lazy and easily distracted by any bright bauble that comes and glitters in the field of my awareness.

I know deep down that to achieve the things I really want, I need to focus on them. The only reason I don't already have them is that I've focused more on other things than on what I now think I want. But changing that focus to the new target, and holding to it, does not happen easily. Somehow, when I want to im-

Seek ye first the good things of the mind, and the rest will either be supplied or its loss will not be felt.

—FRANCIS BACON

Rule your mind or it will rule you.

—HORACE

prove or change things or make something happen, it often feels like I'm stepping into a thick and sluggish world. I'm carving a new path, and it's full of brambles and underbrush. It's a lot easier to think the way I've been thinking, even when I consciously "know better," than to focus consistently along new lines.

We fought so hard against the small things that we became small ourselves.

—EUGENE O'NEILL

So I have tricks. They're all based on a fundamental productivity gimmick: Put things in front of the door. Ever know that you absolutely *have* to take something to work with you the next morning (and your job is at risk if you forget it)? Where did you put it the night before? Right in front of the front door. (For this you got a college degree?) But it *is* a brilliant strategy. You're smart and awake enough the night before to know that in the morning you're barely going to be conscious: "What's *this*? Oh, yeah, I've got to take it with me!"

Become aware of internal, subjective sub-verbal experiences, so that these experiences can be brought into the world of abstraction, of conversation, of naming, etc., with the consequence that it immediately becomes possible for a certain amount of control to be exerted over these hither unconscious and uncontrollable processes.

—ABRAHAM MASLOW

My tricks work the same way. It's just the door of my mind I need to use, not the door of my house—but it's the same idea. If I can put something in front of my consciousness that I know will be good to think about and focus on, constructive thinking will very likely happen. All my projects, my dozens of personal affirmations, my long-term goals, a key thought I captured on a card at a spiritual retreat—all of these are in writing because none are on cruise control, automatically in place, and happening yet in my operational life. I know they probably *will* be at some point down the line, because I know how focus and vision work to unconsciously trigger new perceptions and new behaviors. I just need to get them in front of my face with sufficient regularity. So I've tried to figure out how to have *that* happen in as automatic a way as possible.

Because I'm lazy, not that smart, and still want the best.

By the way . . .

○ What tricks do you use to make yourself more productive?

○ What could you put in front of your mind more regularly that would serve you? Where would you put it?

○ Imagine something you'd like more of today. Have that thought as many times as you can in the next hour.

18.

The clearer your purpose, the more ways to fulfill it.

Here's a fascinating paradox of the material world: The more specific your vision or intention, the more expansive the creativity you will unleash. The more you know why you are doing what you are doing, the more freedom you have to explore all kinds of ways to get there. The clearer it is why you're having the staff party, why you have a den, why you have an assistant, why the software you are designing is needed, and why you are merging with another company, the more you will tap unique ideas, possibilities, and out-of-the-box options for achieving success.

Are You Living in Your Living Room?

THE VALUE OF purposeful focus has been a core element of my learning, teaching, coaching, and management consulting for decades. If we don't know *why* we're doing something, our activities lack meaning, clarity, and direction. If we *do* know the purpose—for a meeting, a brochure, or a company—then we have a criterion for decision making and success in those endeavors, plus the motivation to creatively circumvent obstacles in getting there.

Lately, I've been struck by how many procedures people live and work with that need rethinking. Someone created them at some time, for a good reason perhaps, but that reason is no longer relevant. What triggered this perception for me was seeing some executive offices that were almost totally dysfunctional for personal productivity. There were no places for critical personal-communication supplies, no in- or out-baskets, totally insufficient room for crucial reference files, no printers at hand, no shelf space for useful reference books and manuals. The desktops were huge and gorgeous, but nobody used them, because they might get scratched.

Historically, the purpose of many of these offices was likely to impress people with how much lovely wood the executive could afford and how little he had to work. Wow, look—a throne! Behold—the king! But the people sitting in those offices now have very different priorities and needs: They are there to get work done, to stay on top of a huge workload, to communicate rapidly, and to track things efficiently. Their offices are dinosaurs. They are not serving their new purpose. They should be redesigned.

> *Perfection of means and confusion of goals seem, in my opinion, to characterize our age.*
> —ALBERT EINSTEIN

Over the years in client companies, I've also noticed lots of staff meetings held weekly. They are sometimes only partially attended, with little or no spark. New teams and departments often create weekly meetings because the changes and novelty of their situation demand that they regularly convene to keep everyone on the same page. But after things smooth out and get onto cruise control, the need for weekly powwows slowly ebbs. Yet they keep on meeting, even though it's an ineffective use of people and their time. I believe that every meeting in every organization should be canceled, only those that have a specific purpose should be rescheduled, and the intervals of standing meetings should be set based upon the needs of current reality instead of habit.

One problem with older large sailboats is that the galley is always separated from the group hangout space below, and this layout cramps both spaces. In past decades, most people with big boats could afford to have a full-time crew that prepared and served from the kitchen. New designs, however, catering to modern short-handed sailing, combine the galley and the living area center stage—the same square footage is more comfortable and much better utilized.

The average man does not know what to do with his life, yet wants another one which will last forever.

—ANATOLE FRANCE

Where do most people hang out socially at home? The kitchen. No more maids, no more servants. Today, most of us live another lifestyle entirely, in which we're all in it together, and that's the fun. Observe how many great new restaurants have the cooking center stage! I know some really radical professionals who've turned their living room into their home office! They actually live (socially) in the kitchen and/or den area anyway, so what better place to spend your time working than with lots of light and room for equipment and your library?

Take an inventory of your major assets and procedures—your spaces, your policies, your meetings, your staff, your big toys, your old clothes, and your jewelry. Write down what you consider the purpose(s) for each. I'll bet you'll want to change a number of things, and you'll enjoy doing it.

By the way . . .

○ Which of your routines or procedures feel worn out to you? What would happen if you stopped?

○ What creative use could you make of any unused space in your life?

○ If you created a brand-new office for yourself, what would you keep? What would you eliminate? What would you add?

19.

Best is much better than good.

Commitment to the ultimate quality of anything gives access to unique creativity and intelligence. From the smallest activity to the loftiest goal, an intentional focus on the maximum fulfillment of its purpose generates information and inspiration unavailable from any other perspective.

How to Be Invincible

THERE'S A SIMPLE WAY to become indestructible: Have the intention to do your best at whatever you're doing, right now. To gain the invulnerability I'm referring to, you must pass through the gate of the total vulnerability that putting yourself on that line demands. Not *be* the best—*do* your best. Attempting to be the best can easily have struggle, ego and self-recrimination as baggage, with win/lose as a format. But *doing* your best is a dynamic, ever-changing experience that is possible anytime, by anyone. It's engaging with your life and work in the present, with an attitude and an altitude that are constantly renewing and refreshing. And you can win, whenever.

> *When we do the best we can, we never know what miracle is wrought in our life, or the life of another.*
>
> —HELEN KELLER

The powerful freedom that comes with that experience is not free, however. You must move to a risky edge. You must ask yourself the "what's best?" question, listen inwardly, and muster up the willingness to respond to the answer you get. That might mean sacrificing your momentary pleasure, your habits, your lethargy, and (God forbid!) your self-doubt.

I find it wonderfully ironic that if I'm willing to give up my lust for comfort, my previous independence, and my sense of control to follow the directions of my intuitive guidance, I gain access to a much deeper satisfaction, a real freedom, and true self-empowerment. When I sincerely ask myself, "What is the absolute best thing for me to be doing right now?" and when I'm willing to hear the answer and move on it, I become impervious to the slings and arrows of my own doubt, hesitancy, and self-judgment. No one else knows how to strike at me with the sly vengeance of my own negative self. When I truly focus on doing the best I can, however, I have (at least for the moment) forgotten and forgiven the past and dropped the fears of the future. That in itself is certainly a healthy (if not a miraculously healing) event.

> *The master in the art of living makes little distinction between his work and his play, his labor and his leisure, his mind and his body, his information and his recreation, his love and his religion. He hardly knows which is which. He simply pursues his vision of excellence at whatever he does, leaving others to decide whether he is working or playing. To him he's always doing both.*
>
> —JAMES MICHENER

What is best for you to be doing right now? You can move on that answer in whatever activity at whatever level you find yourself. Best does not mean perfect—it simply means best. The best you can do in this moment, with whatever awareness and resources you can muster right now. Make the best spaghetti sauce you can with what you have and who you are, right now. Make this the best staff meeting you could possibly have, given the circumstances at the moment. While talking with your friend, your spouse, your mom, or your son, make it the very best conversation that you could be having. The best proposal, the best drive with my family, the best perform- ance review, and the best nap.

It's interesting that the answers I get when I'm smart enough to manage my life this way are never very far from what I've actually

been doing. But the shift in perspective always creates ideas and in-
clinations that add to my productivity, whether that's more business for my business or just more joy in my day.

By the way . . .
○ When you ask yourself what's the best thing you could
be doing at this moment, what's the answer? (If it's not
reading this . . . shall I see you another time?!)
○ What might prevent you from asking and answering that
question?

20.

A change in focus equals a change in result.

If you want different results, a change of focus is required. Once you shift the image held in your mind, different things will automatically start to happen. Focus on red, red shows up. Focus on a different outcome for a conversation, and different thoughts will come to you. Focus on seeing a specific new car model, and it will be as if a ship just unloaded a bunch of them all over the freeway. Your brain has an in-built mechanism for finding patterns you've programmed because of where you've put your attention. Solutions, innovations, and success come not from greater intelligence or creativity but from what we notice because of where we point those attributes.

Are You Ready for "Ready"?

Quiet minds cannot be perplexed or frightened, but go on in fortune or misfortune at their own private pace, like a clock during a thunderstorm.

—ROBERT LOUIS STEVENSON

ONE SUBTLE LIFE SKILL should become part of the competency set for all professionals (and all people): How fast can you get back to "ready"? How easily and rapidly can you relax and refocus when it's necessary to do so? How good are you at creating a centered, balanced, aware, and open state of mind for the next input or impetus that emerges in your world? When something pushes your button, rings your bell, grabs your attention, bothers, upsets, engrosses, or excites you, what is your lag time to unhook from those feelings, clear the decks internally, and engage again appropriately with a fresh perspective and with the new subject/object that must now be confronted?

How can you develop a personal system that fosters a life-and-work-style that can consistently and easily be returned to "ready"? The static and backed-up energy created by undecided, unorganized, incomplete stuff on your desk, in your office, and in your head generates a psychic backwater that undermines the ability to easily be in that state. It's like trying to survey the swamp when you're being sucked into the quicksand.

In tennis, when you're waiting for the serve, what is the best frame of mind, emotional state, and physical position to be in? In karate, when three people are approaching you from different sides and preparing to attack, what's the most effective stance to take? When the final negotiation is in progress for an acquisition and their lawyer tosses out a surprising and potentially deal-breaking requirement, how many of your internal resources are available to make rapid intuitive decisions? Can you let go of the choke hold on your assumptions or projections and take new actions based on an intelligently fresh perspective? Can you surrender control at one level, in order to move quickly to the higher one?

The next time you want to hire someone and are evaluating performance and skill sets, look at the person's ability to get ready fast. When has she been really surprised (positively or negatively)? How long did it take her to integrate it and navigate a positive response? This behavior is going to be valued and promoted by your organi-

The mere formulation of a problem is far more essential than its solution, which may be merely a matter of mathematical or experimental skills. To raise new questions, new possibilities, to regard old problems from a new angle requires creative imagination and marks real advances in science.

—ALBERT EINSTEIN

For piety lies not in being often seen turning a veiled head to stones, nor in approaching every altar, nor in lying prostrate . . . before the temples of the gods, nor in sprinkling altars with the blood of beasts . . . but rather in being able to look upon all things with a mind at peace.

—LUCRETIUS

zation. The next time you're assessing your own strong and weak suits, focus on the same question. How ready for "ready" are you? Twenty years from now, you'll be glad you did.

I'm working now with a new and vital affirmation in my own self-development process: "Relax, refocus." Try it out.

By the way . . .

○ What's your biggest problem or issue right now? How are you focusing on it? What image are you holding about it?

○ How easily can you drop any thoughts you have right now and focus on wild success?

○ How would you like to feel and respond when you get your next big surprise?

21.

Perspective is the most valuable commodity on the planet.

This is the corollary to the principle "A change in focus equals a change in results." The priorities of your current job (and the actions you focus on) may shift if you think about what your job needs to be eighteen months from now. Putting things in a different context can generate unrealized ideas and solutions. Your point of view can change the most drastic of circumstances into the most powerful of positive experiences. An infinite number of things in the universe are held back from you only by your altitude and attitude.

Bootstrapping Yourself into Better

SOMETIMES I'M NOT AS SMART as I am at other times. And most of the time, I'm not as inspired as I want to be. So if I really want to improve my work, my life, and myself—and if I'm really as lazy as I pretend to be—the smartest thing to do is to capture thoughts and expressions of ideas and experiences when I'm in a more elevated state of awareness. Then I can use those triggers to inform, lift, and direct myself when I'm not so sharp.

This means capturing an idea that might be useful when I have that idea, because it might not come again. If I'm on the beach and think about a

> *Life is a series of inspired follies. The difficulty is to find them to do. Never lose a chance. It doesn't come every day.*
>
> —GEORGE BERNARD SHAW

new way to emphasize a point in my seminars, I need to write it down as soon as I'm near a pen and paper. When I'm driving in the car and think about a really creative and loving thing to do for somebody, I need to note it right away on a pad or a tape. When I'm in a state of consciousness more sublime than usual, I need to express it by writing out an affirmation or inspired thought.

It is our relation to circumstances that determines their influence over us. The same wind that carries one vessel into port may blow another off shore.
—CHRISTIAN BOVÉE

But the tricky thing is that when I'm having those thoughts, I often don't think I need to do anything with them, to make use of them. There's something so "of course" about them while I'm having them that I'm sure I'll never forget them and that I'll have them when I need them. Of course, two minutes later, when I'm thinking about the next positive, useful thing, which I'm sure I'll never forget, I've forgotten the first one! And when I'm in positive states of mind, it seems as if the world will always be that way, so there's no need to prepare for when it's not. But just because we can be thoughtful, smart, and inspired, that does not make us that way all the time.

I can alter my life by altering my attitude. He who would have nothing to do with thorns must never attempt to gather flowers.
—HENRY DAVID THOREAU

If you're like me, you need to create and use your bootstraps well. When I'm doing errands or surfing the Web, it's good to be reminded of what I wanted to get for someone when I was more thoughtful. When I'm making a point in a seminar, it's good to be reminded of the creative idea I had about how to explain something while I was walking on the beach. And when I'm in the doldrums, it's great to pull out my set of personal affirmations and read through them, to lift my focus and energy.

So when you are inspired, leverage it to the hilt. Careful—happy can happen anytime. Develop the habit and find the tools you need to grab the goodies when you get them. Then bring the results back in front of you when you can best make use of them.

By the way . . .

○ How can you best take advantage of your most challenging situation right now?

○ What is the most inspiring thing you've written or read recently? How could you glean even more value from it?

○ What's the best thing that's happened to you in the last few days? What could you do to get something like it to happen again?

22.

You have to think about your stuff more than you think.

Whatever we've let into our inner or outer environment that doesn't belong where it is the way it is needs to have something done about it. What has to happen to move toward closure is not immediately evident just because the e-mail, letter, idea, or situation is there. We have to think. Not much, but enough to decide what the very next action is that's required to kick-start the process toward completion. That thinking is often avoided, until the pressure mounts for us to finally have to deal with it. Minimally requisite thinking about stuff doesn't take much time and effort (usually about fifteen seconds). But it does take time and effort.

Productivity Doesn't Happen by Itself

THERE ARE THREE THINGS that have to happen in order for us to define our work and be maximally productive about it. And these three things don't happen by themselves. We have to train ourselves to do all three, and until we establish them as automatic and habitual behaviors, we have to discipline ourselves to get them done.

We have to:

1. Make decisions about what we are going to do with our stuff and the next actions required to do it (what would "doing" look like?). Stuff is unactionable until we've decided the outcome and the next step to move toward it. Things on lists and in

stacks and e-mail generally repel instead of attract us to get involved, until we know exactly what our intention is about them and whether the next step is to make a call, draft a response, buy nails, talk to . . . and so on.

2. Write down those outcomes and actions, if we don't do them in the moment we think of them. Even if we decide what we need to do about something and file it in psychic RAM, we run serious risk of losing sight of the option and creating instant failure and unnecessary stress. That part of us thinks we should be doing everything in there all at once.

3. Look at the reminders (when we could effectively move on them). Even if you've decided that the next step is sending an e-mail, if you don't look at the reminder when you're online, you risk missing an opportunity to move something forward now. When you're in a certain context, to be the most efficient, you need to see all the things that could be done in that context.

These three behaviors combined are a master skill set for knowledge work. Yet virtually everyone I come across in the professional world could significantly improve how consistently he or she does these three critical productivity activities.

We were not taught these skills growing up. The workaday world of our parents did not require these critical behaviors of knowledge work. People just showed up and did what obviously needed doing—they could see it in front of them. Few people work in that kind of world anymore. Anyone these days just showing up and expecting

An hour of effective, precise, hard, disciplined, and integrated thinking can be worth a month of hard work. Thinking is the very essence of, and the most difficult thing to do in, business and life. Empire builders spend hour after hour on mental work . . . while others party. If you're not consciously aware of putting forth the effort to exert self-guided integrated thinking, if you don't act beyond your feelings and you take the path of least resistance, then you're giving in to laziness and no longer control your life.
—DAVID KEKICH

The ancestor of every action is a thought.
—RALPH WALDO EMERSON

Think like a man of action, act like a man of thought.

—HENRI BERGSON

to work on what's visibly been put in front of him is hoping for a retro world that doesn't exist. That person is likely to be experiencing mounting stress that won't be getting any better. We must train ourselves to apply our mental horsepower to actually know what it *is*, exactly, that is in front of us and therefore how it can be dispatched.

By the way . . .

○ What issue is taking up space in your psyche? What's the next action on it, and where could that happen? Where can you put a reminder of the action? (How long did this process take?)

○ What can you see in your immediate environment that doesn't belong there permanently? What thinking is required to know what to do with it?

23.

You don't have to think about your stuff as much as you're afraid you might.

This is the corollary to the previous principle. Though you need to reflect about your stuff to know what to do with it, it's not as much as you likely feel it might be. A little bit of thinking ("What's my intention? What's my next action?") creates relaxed focus and control. But most people resist thinking at all about many things. Why? Because their minds are so quick and sophisticated that they glance at a situation and freak themselves out with all the intricate details of what they're afraid they'd have to think about—if they thought about it. So it has a piece of them, psychologically. Decide the outcome and the action step, put reminders of those somewhere your brain trusts you'll see them at the right time, and listen to your brain breathe easier: "Ah, done . . . for now."

Being Complete with Your Incompletions

IN SEMINARS, I often show people all my projects (about 60 at this writing) and next actions to do about them (about 150) on a screen. Often someone will say, "How do you keep from being totally overwhelmed and discouraged when you constantly look at all those things to do?" They're really saying, "I don't want to have to do that!"

This probably stems from their innate desire for some internal peace, balance, and at-one-ness with their world and themselves. Reminding themselves of all the

Ever stop to think and forget to start again?

—UNKNOWN

open loops of their life—all their "work"—seems to most people disturbing to the tranquillity of Just Being. But it's not. As a matter of fact, it makes for a fuller expression of that harmony. You just need to be complete with your incompletions.

Thought is useful when it motivates for action, and a hindrance when it substitutes for action.
—BILL RAEDER

A paradox is at play here, for sure. If you consciously capture, track, review, and renegotiate all your commitments to yourself and others, they are, in a sense, *done.* There is no residue, no distraction, and no pervasive angst from having attached your energies to unseen and unremembered agreements. You look at them all in the light of day (and the light of your conscious awareness) and say, "Well, I previously said I would do this, and I still want to do it as soon as I can, but *not at this moment.*"

The one important thing I have learned over the years is the difference between taking one's work seriously and taking one's self seriously. The first is imperative and the second is disastrous.
—MARGOT FONTEYN

The people who think that my lists of things to accomplish are burdensome have a lot of work they just don't want to look at. And what they resist, they're stuck with. I consistently come back to the awareness that I'm not my work, because I've objectified and reviewed it. I think many people still have a hard time telling the difference.

Making the simple complicated is commonplace; making the complicated simple, awesomely simple—that's creativity.
—CHARLES MINGUS

Truly being "at one with the universe" frankly has very little to do with keeping lists or not, being productive or not, or even having a clear mind, balanced emotions, or a vibrant body. If you're good at it, you can be "at one" with confusion, stress, the flu, and even negative cash flow. You can surrender up the burdens and attachments of your life at any moment to what you relate to as the higher power at work and be free in consciousness.

But if you avoid or ineffectively manage your incompletions, you'll probably be forced to confront more negative experiences than you would like.

I don't teach how to be "spiritual." I teach how to clear and manage focus so the energy you have is most efficiently used, to get what that energy can produce.

By the way . . .

○ How did you feel about your work the week before your vacation? Why?

○ What are you procrastinating about that seems too complex for your brain to deal with comfortably? What could you do as a next physical action to start a core dump from your head about it?

24.

If you know what you're doing, efficiency is the only improvement opportunity.

Once a purpose, goal, or standard is clear, the best you can do is get there and maintain it with as little effort as possible. Energy is not wasted, and your resources are optimally freed for more of what you want or want to do.

Stress Transcendence

MANY OF THE CONCEPTS and models I teach relieve the unproductive pressure in our lives—the unnecessary stress created by commitments that are allowed to take up residence in our psyche and then create inappropriate demands on our energy and focus. By themselves these methods work—to a point. But whether they *really* work in the long run depends ultimately on why I'm doing them. Why, really, am I clearing my decks of psychic rubble?

> There are only two ways to live your life. One is as though nothing is a miracle. The other is as though everything is a miracle.
>
> —ALBERT EINSTEIN

If I'm managing the incompletions of my world because in truth I simply want to disengage from my life, the stress never really goes away. Oh, sure, I can get a grosser level of relief—and sometimes lots of it. It's great to get my head empty, my in-box cleaned up, and my project and action lists updated. But after all that, a part of me can still want to check out, leave, go numb, or in some way blot out the deeper noise that's still there. It's not a big, traumatic, or obviously negative thing I'm avoiding. If it were, it would probably be easier to identify. It's a low-level incessant buzzing that seems to infuse everything with dullness. I experience things coming into my world as irritations, not opportunities. I can't wait to "finish"—so that I can go do something to escape from the whole process! But inevitably with that approach, defeatism creeps in: Why should I even start when there's never any finish? Whoops. Now, that's a negative self-fulfilling loop in my mind if there ever was one!

It is only when we realize that life is taking us nowhere that it begins to have meaning.

—P. D. OUSPENSKY

If, however, I'm able to move my inner awareness to a more spiritually connected place, more from my heart than my head, it's a totally different game. It's the same activity, but it's draped in elegance and ease. There's an acceptance of whatever is in front of me, and I'm curious about its possibilities. There's an interest in processing all my stuff with our workflow methods because it deserves that—or rather, because *I* deserve it. When the fulfillment is present inside me and I'm okay with myself at the deepest level, it's not about getting everything done. It's just a process of doing—and a very conscious process at that. What am I doing now, and now, and now, and now . . . ? And is this the best way to be doing it?

Progress is made by lazy men looking for easier ways to do things.

—ROBERT HEINLEIN

Before undergoing a surgical operation, arrange your temporal affairs. You may live.

—AMBROSE BIERCE

The wonderful paradox is that the more I get attracted to focusing on the outer physical world (and everything that goes with it), the more I find myself attempting to escape the slings and arrows of that materiality. The more spiritually I'm focused and the less attached to the physical I become, the more productively engaged I seem to be within the material world. I have a clearer sense of where things fit for me in the grander scheme, and I don't allow myself the laxness of being irresponsible for the smallest details about things and activities.

Sure, this is just another version of a simple truth: Clarity of purpose is necessary in order to know how to evaluate the experiences and possibilities moving my way. But lately, I've been coming to know this on a whole new level. The difference, it seems, is beginning to really *be* the purpose instead of just having one.

We have infinite trouble in solving man-made mysteries; it is only when we set out to discover the secret of God that our difficulties disappear.

—MARK TWAIN

Easy? Once I'm there, in that lovely state of simultaneous being and doing, it seems that it didn't require any effort at all. It's timeless and there's no "effort-ing." How does one get into that state, and how long does it take to get there? All I really know is that it's always available to me, when I'm available to it.

By the way . . .

○ When have you improved your efficiency with something? How did that feel? Why did you do that?

○ What do you think you need to organize better that you keep procrastinating about? What would you be able to do—or do better—if you had that handled?

25.

Only one thing on your mind is "in the zone."

If you are conscious, you cannot have an empty mind—it will always be focused on something. But if it has only one thing as a focus, with no inner distraction or conflict, you will be "in your zone." Then, in a sense, nothing you do will be any more or less significant than anything else. Everything will be equally all-encompassing and important. There will be no distinction between work and play, intense or relaxed. It's all the same. It will always be, simply, "What's now, and what's next?"

How Important Is Anything but the Most Important Thing?

AT ANY MOMENT, giving full attention to the one thing at hand is a hallmark of high performance. This is relatively easy when you're totally engaged with something as an unmistakable top priority. You can get to be in that place for both proactive and reactive reasons. You may have so identified with what you want to accomplish that nothing could deter your attention from the topmost issue. Or there is such an obvious crisis at hand that you absolutely *must* allocate all your psychic forces to deal with it.

While people are in either of those circumstances, they are unlikely to be very concerned with all the other incompletions of their life and work. They will tend to be totally engrossed in what's happening here and now. The art would be to stay in that zone all the time—to keep the appropriate amount of attention focused on the most appropriate thing, from the most appropriate perspective, for the appropriate length of time. No more, no less. Then refocus on the next thing, in the same way, with 100 percent positive creative energy.

The affairs of life embrace a multitude of interests, and he who reasons in any one of them, without consulting the rest, is a visionary unsuited to control the business of the world.

—JAMES FENIMORE COOPER

This would be a Zen-like state of productivity, in which you deal with what's present from a perspective that is both detached and fully engaged. It's the ultimate executive style—show up, integrate, think, decide, and dispatch, intelligently informed by internalized outcomes, visions, and standards. You worry about nothing before, nothing after. Clean, clear, precise, with no residue. No ripples left in the water. "Who *was* that masked man?!"

But how do you get there? And once there, how do you keep yourself there? It has a lot to do with trusting a bigger game and with your ability to identify with it. Also with being totally true to your own agreements with yourself, which can exist at multiple levels of your existence and can be very subtle.

There is one thing we can do, and the happiest people are those who do it to the limit of their ability. We can be completely present. We can be all here. We can . . . give all our attention to the opportunity before us.

—MARK VAN DOREN

Can you truly manifest that clarity of focus if there are any incompletions left not completely managed and renegotiated with yourself? Is sacrificing less-than-immediately-critical details the ultimate way to experience the richness of life? Or is it a temporary cure, which avoids responsibility for commitments that at some point will come back to haunt you? I've coached many executive types who don't consciously think of themselves as "stressed." But without exception, when they capture, clarify, and organize all their open loops in a contained, objective system, they "feel a lot better." So what did they feel before? Good? Maybe, but obviously not as good as they could.

How important is it to have handled all the other stuff except what you're doing right now, in order to be 100 percent available for what you're doing right now? Is it really possible to block out everything and not be affected by anything but the one thing you're focused on in the moment? Obviously your conscious mind can be aware of only a relatively few things at any point in time, and the rest is on some psychological shelf somewhere. But can you really compartmentalize your psyche so that you are truly not in any way negatively affected by any of the other aspects of your life and work that are not clear, not decided, not organized as effectively as they could be?

What does it take to absolutely trust yourself and what you're doing—all the time?

By the way . . .

○ When did you last experience being "in the zone"? Do you know how you got there?

○ What's keeping you from being totally present today, with whatever you're doing? What could you do to handle that?

○ Do you ever find yourself doing things to avoid doing something else?

26.

The value of a future goal is the present change it fosters.

A vision of a desired future allows you to focus immediately on an improved condition. It changes what you perceive and how you perform—now. Its value is not actually about achieving something in time, but rather about how it changes the substance and quality of the decisions you're making in this moment. It affects what you choose to perceive, feel, and do in the present. Imagining a positive outcome forward in time provides a believability of the scenario and matures the consciousness. In spite of ourselves, we begin to act as if it has truth.

To Do or to Be? Or Is That the Question?

THERE'S A WONDERFUL DILEMMA in the exploration of our human purpose and therefore our ultimate "success." Are we to be or to do? Does our highest achievement spring from a renunciation of material striving and an enlightened connection with our spiritual source? Or does human fulfillment come from accomplishment, from making things happen for us and for others in this world?

Intuitively I know that it is a false dichotomy. It is not an either/or proposition. Real being is a highly dynamic and active experience, which may or may not include physical endeavor. Successful, quality "doing"

> You've got to think about big things while you're doing small things so that all the small things go in the right direction.
>
> —ALVIN TOFFLER

is fulfilling in itself, with a timeless and Zen-like aspect, often associated with higher states of consciousness ("in the zone"). In their positive aspects, doing and being seem to coexist very nicely.

I arise in the morning torn between a desire to improve (or save) the world and a desire to enjoy (or savor) the world. This makes it hard to plan the day.
—E. B. WHITE

But it's a subtle business. The inner reflective focus and the outer expression and manifestation *are* different processes and can be experienced as mutually exclusive. If I need to nurture my being and I'm just busily doing, out of habit or nervousness from my inner disquiet, my activity is hollow, tiring, and unfulfilling. Conversely, if I really ought to be doing and I'm just trying to "be" as a way to avoid my physical commitments, my beingness is disturbed, and it's almost impossible to give my attention to my spiritual or higher process.

Make no little plans; they have no magic to stir men's blood and probably in themselves will not be realized. Make big plans; aim high in hope and work remembering that a noble, logical diagram once recorded will never die.
—DANIEL HUDSON BURNHAM

So there is an issue—or a dualistic aspect of our desire for human perfection or at least progress—that begs for resolution. But I learned years ago that in this kind of no-win philosophical situation, there is probably a higher perspective that dissolves, rather than resolves, the dissonance. In other words, being versus doing may not be the issue.

We are multidimensional beings. A part of us exists in dimensions that seem outside space and time. Physical activity has very little, if anything, to do with those aspects of who we are and how we connect with them. And yet simultaneously we still have a large part of our selves invested in a world that by its nature is in constant change and motion.

For the parts of us operating on this level, the key issue is not *whether* we are active but *how.* If you are conscious at all, you cannot be inactive. You are active by the nature of your intention of where and how you focus your consciousness. "Being" is a highly active process, but the movement is internal instead of outwardly focused. Though someone is "meditative" and quiet, they have merely lessened the distractions of the outer world to enable the awareness of much subtler levels of inner experience.

If the success or failure of this planet and of human beings depended on how I am and what I do, how would I be and what would I do?

—BUCKMINSTER FULLER

Perhaps the questions really should be these: Where is the balance between my shoulder-to-the-wheel hard work and my inner reflective process that nourishes and rekindles the flame of inspiration and expansive expression? Are my inner-focused and outer-focused activities in proper proportion and relation to each other? What *type* of action is optimal for me right now? Is it best to take time to breathe, refocus in a subtler place, and shift to a higher and healthier perspective? Or do I need to put my physical butt in gear and get moving, to keep my agreements with myself and expand my expression in the world with more gusto and conscious involvement?

To be or to do is not the issue. The question is this: "What type of doing most aligns me with my being?"

By the way . . .

○ Imagine yourself wildly successful, five years from now. How would that feel? How would you relate with the world around you? Try it today.

○ Do you feel in balance with your inner and outer worlds? If not, what would bring them more into balance?

PART III

CREATE STRUCTURES THAT WORK

or

It's Hard to Stay on Track Without Rails

We don't feel constrained by the limitations that really work for us. We're grateful for the lines down the middle of the road—they give us the freedom to get places fast with a minimum of stress and risk. Effective forms don't take space—they create it. At times, tightening up our systems is what's needed to release new levels of output and expression.

27.

Stability on one level opens creativity on another.

We live and work on many different levels all the time. When one level is disturbed, it pulls energy and focus from the others, until it is resolved. When things are in balance, a natural and sustainable flow of creative energy becomes accessible throughout all endeavors.

Organization and Creativity: Friends or Foes?

I FIND IT INTERESTING how many people still think organization and creativity are mutually exclusive: "Don't bother me about getting organized and with all those lists—I just want to be creative." Or "I don't need all that organization stuff—I can keep everything in my head." Why do people think that "getting organized" is antithetical to spontaneity, intuition, and freedom? Probably because they don't identify strongly enough with a desired experience or outcome in that particular area of their life. When you really want to have or experience something, what you know you must do to get there is seldom viewed as "getting organized." It is just done. When you "have to get organized," you're probably not appropriately invested yet in what you need to get organized for.

> *I'd like people to remember me for a diligent expert workman. I think a poet is a workman. Shakespeare was a workman. And God's a workman. I don't think there's anything better than a workman.*
> —LAURENCE OLIVIER

If you want to express yourself on canvas, and oil paints are

*Get your beingness
perfected so that the
routine of your life
does not distract you
or disturb you and so
you can maintain a
state of loving in
everything you do.
Then you can expand
the scope of your
activity, moving your
loving heart out to
others in a natural,
ordinary way.*

—JOHN-ROGER

your medium, you will organize your paints and brushes. You won't think about "getting organized"—you'll just do it. If you want to catch fish, and really enjoy the sport, you will maintain your lures and line in some organized fashion. The best at it will always have their tackle ready.

Why is that not often true about all the pieces and parts of someone's work? I've met many a senior professional who would maintain an excruciatingly shipshape navigation station on his sailboat but have an e-mail in-basket that was totally out of control. Why? What's the difference, ultimately?

Once you taste what it's like to operate with a clear head (I mean a *really* clear head), I doubt that you will spend much energy thinking about "having to get organized." You'll just do it so you can maintain that experience. Compared to the West, the Far East has a very different model for the path to spontaneity. In the Far East, if you want to know true freedom of expression, you may be expected to dedicate a lifetime to rigorous simplicity and discipline.

It's hard to be fully creative without structure and constraint. Try to paint without a canvas. Creativity and freedom are two sides of the same coin. I like the best of both worlds. Want freedom? Get organized. Want to be organized? Get creative.

By the way . . .
○ Where in your life and work would an objective observer think you were "organized"? What is it that you care about that gets you to do that?
○ Where do you think you are "disorganized"? What outcome, that calls for more organization, would make this area of your life more important or interesting?

28.

Form and function must match
for maximum productivity.

*The difference between structures that support and those that constrict
is simply their alignment with the purpose. Meetings scheduled too
frequently for what they are trying to accomplish will be unattractive
and unattended. Organizations inappropriately defined for projected
growth will create bottlenecks. A hallmark of master craftspeople is their
knowledge of what tool is best for what job.*

The Visionary and the Doer—a Personal Division of Labor

I'VE REALIZED LATELY that there are two distinctly different hats
that I wear internally as I move forward in my life: the Visionary
and the Doer. They think and act differently, and things work a lot
better when I don't get their roles and responsibilities confused.

I've known for years that individuals have personality and work
styles that range on this continuum—there are "blue sky" thinkers
who hate details and commitments, and there are implementers
who get extremely uncomfortable when asked to make up something or pick a direction. I'm now clear that I have both in my internal committee.

My Visionary is the one who loves just to hang out under the
oaks, sipping a cup of coffee, getting inspired with great new projects and ideal scenarios. It even thinks strategically from time to

time. My Doer, however, is most engaged when it's picking up something out of my in-basket, deciding on and completing a simple action step that concretely makes progress on what's right in front of it. As long as they don't get in each other's face, we're cool.

A vision without a task is but a dream; a task without a vision is drudgery; a vision and a task is the hope of the world.

—FROM A CHURCH IN SUSSEX, ENGLAND, C. 1730

But when I'm in Visionary mode and I start thinking about how I ought to finish up all the stuff I've created and how much work I've generated for myself, I get resentful and withdrawn. And when I'm into Doing and completing and I allow the self-talk to creep in that I "should be doing and thinking about more important and bigger things," I emotionally deflate and just want to numb out.

Here's what makes this inner partnership work the best:

1. *My in-basket.* When I'm in creative mode, I can just toss an idea onto my notepad or into the in-tray—into "the system," delegating it immediately to "someone else." My Doer will pick it up and ask, "What's the next action?" and then make something happen.
2. *My projects and someday/maybe lists.* They are trophy cases for the Visionary.
3. *My next-actions lists.* They give my Doer little "widgets" to crank, about which it can feel productive and successful quickly.
4. *The Weekly Review.* It's the way I get the Visionary and the Doer together in a regular staff meeting, and they get to work things out with cooperation and enthusiasm.

By the way . . .

○ Which part of you is dominant, the Visionary or the Doer?

○ What could you do to support the weaker part?

29.

Your system has to be better than your mind for your mind to let go.

You can't fool your mind. It's an expert on your current personal management system, and it knows whether you can be trusted to look at what you need to at the appropriate time. It knows if you've decided what the next action should be. And it knows if there is a reminder of that action placed somewhere that you will actually look, when you could possibly take that action. If you have not done any of that, your mind won't let go. It can't. It will endlessly keep trying to remind you of what to remember. The mind is a loyal and dedicated servant, but it needs to be given the jobs it does well—not the ones that it mismanages.

Can Your Mind Keep Its New Job?

GETTING EVERYTHING OUT of your head and making decisions about what it all means to you and what you need to do to move everything forward will give a tremendous freedom to your head. Without exception, when anyone actually does this in a complete way, his or her mental and intuitive focus lights up and lifts up, and things are seen and experienced from a new and healthy perspective. It's like a helium balloon that automatically rises when released. Fresh ideas show up, and a more executive point of view is at hand to deal with all the stuff as it comes at us willy-nilly. The mind graduates to a new level of functioning. But this promotion can be short-lived.

It's one thing for your mental focus to get a higher-level job, and it's quite another for it to keep that job. Your mind can stay at the new horizon only if the levels below it continue to be handled effectively. Doing proactive knowledge work (thinking, deciding, and sorting) and setting up a well-organized personal-management system to handle the results is like hiring a fabulous executive assistant for yourself—it releases you to do the really important things you want to focus on. But if that system is not consistently reviewed and kept current, it's like having your key support staff quit without notice or replacement. You're immediately dragged down again to worrying about who's picking up the phone, where are the tickets, what appointments do I have tomorrow, did we ever get back to Sean about the proposal? And that's not what you were hired to do. But if that level is not handled, you can't really *do* what you were hired to do—at least not at a maximal level of functioning.

This constant, unproductive preoccupation with all the things we have to do is the single largest consumer of time and energy.
—KERRY GLEESON

Once all your projects and related actions have been clarified and determined, those lists must be kept current and complete. To maintain the benefits of a clear head and heightened responsiveness, to keep balanced and stay totally focused on the real opportunities, you must care for and feed your placeholders for your commitments still at hand—your lists. The positive experience goes away if the system and the process that created it fall behind, and that can happen quickly. Within days (sometimes hours), new input must be integrated into your mix, details need to be checked on and wrapped up, and ends will have become loose that need to be tracked and managed. You've got to get back to squeaky-clean again, in terms of what you're doing and what you're *not* doing. Your mind must stay engaged with the system in order to transcend the level the system is managing.

The palest ink is clearer than the fondest memory.
—CHINESE SAYING

Over the years, we have discovered that what we call the "weekly review"—catching up with all your capturing, processing, and organizing—is the most critical habit to build, to ensure that relaxed control is a way of life instead of an exceptional experience. There seems to be something in our psyche that maps nicely to a seven-day cycle for our operational work life. We need to back off every seven days or so from our tree hugging and do a little forest management—not in the lofty clouds but at the level of the projects and activities we have in front of us for the next short period of time.

This kind of functional overviewing of *everything* on our plates does not happen of its own accord. It requires a discipline of logistical focus to bracket one to two hours at the end of a workweek, to back out of the daily grind just enough to get control of it. And most people behave as if this kind of review were an offline, nice-to-do-but-I-don't-have-time-to type of thing. What many don't realize is that it is the only way to stop thinking about how you should be thinking about what you should be thinking about. You can actually finish that exercise and quiet that nagging part of your mind. But it takes about one to two hours weekly—for the rest of your life.

By the way . . .
○ When did you last complete a total review of all your outstanding projects and next actions?
○ What could you do to ensure that you do that more consistently?

30.

Response ability improves viability.

Anything that can enhance your awareness of the environment, speed up your response time, and balance your internal system (to eliminate over- and underreactions) will provide competitive advantage and improve performance. Sensitivity to input with adaptability to change contributes to the survival of a species, a fighter pilot, and a product line.

The Disorder Drug

MOST DRUGS—pharmaceutical or recreational—buffer us temporarily from reality. They desensitize our reactions to invading foreign bodies (such as bacteria and bosses). Piles of unprocessed stuff can easily perform the same function.

People can dampen down their relationship to the world by allowing lots of undecided things to mount up into a fortress around them. Any input from the outside must then weave its way past the barricades of paper, hundreds of e-mails, and misplaced information and commitments. The syndrome feeds on itself. As disorder grows, it creates increasing "wiggle room" for unpleasant or challenging things to get shunted into the background and ignored. And this process is not always embar-

People are lonely because they build walls instead of bridges.

—W. E. CHANNING

Blessed are the flexible, for they shall not be bent out of shape.

—DR. MICHAEL MCGRIFFY

rassing—"overwhelmingly busy" can seem to equal "important" in the workplace.

It's nice to get some protection from the onslaughts of our life and work. But drugs create addictions and artificial responses and can be tough habits to break. Even when people decide to "dry out," cleaning up their environment internally and externally, the new experience will likely allow a feeling of vulnerability to creep in that seems raw and uncomfortable. Ask anyone who's ever gone cold turkey. To have no subtle excuse anymore to avoid responding to the transactions of life and work can make you feel naked, until you're used to it.

If our work environment is easily understood, even by strangers, . . . it also makes it easier to collect the wisdom of everyone.

—KIO SUZAKI

But you can get clean and get used to that, too. Letting things lie around unprocessed can start to feel more uncomfortable than dealing with them. This may be an addiction, too, but it's one that generates healthier and more productive consequences.

Those of us who've spent thousands of hours helping people shift to a more complete and more front-end decision-making personal model have seen amazing improvements in teams and whole organizational cultures. We do this by working one at a time with the individuals involved. A majority of the problems for which managers often think they need "team-building" exercises simply go away because the nervous system of the organism has become more refined. It has moved up the food chain.

The problem is never how to get new, innovative thoughts into your mind, but how to get the old ones out. Every mind is a building filled with archaic furniture. Clean out a corner of your mind and creativity will instantly fill it.

—DEE HOCK

By the way . . .

○ Anything you're avoiding responding to in your environment? What would it take to handle it?

○ What medium do people most trust to use to communicate with you? Why?

31.

Your system is only as good as its weakest link.

The value of a personal-management system is its ability to release resources for higher and better work, because of the trust its support provides to the psyche. But no system is truly effective if there is any inconsistency in that support. The commander will always have to handle an unmanned post. If no one has been duly charged with ensuring clean toilets, the CEO will ultimately have to do it. A system relieves no pressure unless it truly handles its job 100 percent. And though it's easy to create fancy systems in concept, software, and seminars, how will they work when you have the flu and feel awful? Real systems must be solid enough to hold up in the toughest reality—when we least feel like maintaining them.

How Is Your Wiring Firing?

ORGANIZATIONS HAVE NERVES and central nervous systems, which always reflect their weakest link. If someone on a team doesn't respond to e-mails for two weeks, the entire group's sensitivity and efficiency have been dulled. If everyone deals with his or her communications within a few hours, high productivity usually occurs. People often bitch about the load of seemingly nonpurposeful e-mails they get from their organization, but those who complain about e-mail the most are usually the ones who make the worst use of it. Dullness in the system begets dullness in the system.

Interactions in this environment become thick and sluggish. Other people must raise the noise of their communications to get through these buffer zones. The increased (and often inappropriate) volume and urgency foster a reactive atmosphere, and the culture gets on edge. Organizations become simultaneously dulled and hyperactive. Critical strategic change initiatives broadcast into the culture go into one side of the swamp but don't come out the other. Purposeless messages get free rein without consequences, and a cry-wolf mentality numbs the communication senses.

The real challenge is to make good communication a handy and well-used tool. Then you are likely to pick it up and use it without thinking.
—MAX DEPREE

On the other side of the equation are individuals and teams who keep their e-mail and other communications processed and emptied regularly. They've moved on to much more mature problems. They're skilled at rapid dispatch—whether it's important or junk mail. Yet what's more interesting is that they just don't seem to experience as much irrelevant stuff. They have, by their consistent behavior, created an aura of sensitive responsiveness to the network they're connected to. When people know that you're paying close attention to what they send you, they can't help but be more conscious of the quality and appropriateness of their messages. When the feedback loop is shortened in any relationship, it breeds a much healthier and more productive situation. It's more refined, in the best sense of that word.

When that happens in an organizational culture (families included), all systems are positively affected. Immediate responsiveness with increased but balanced sensitivity shortens all the cycle times for communications and decision making. There are no short circuits or blown fuses. Distracting, irrelevant, and toxic content becomes obvious and finds no backwater in which to fester.

In our work, when we happen to coach all members of a group in the workflow process, we teach them to create a response *now*, so they can stop thinking about what they should be thinking about. Doing nothing is not only a waste of energy—it often promotes decay and unnecessary complexity and stress. We demonstrate how conscious action is better than unconscious reaction. This is not promoting knee-jerk reactions. Thoughtfulness in the communication is not eliminated but refined and enhanced. Because the interaction is happening *before* things get into crisis mode, it is more conscious and proactive. In this way, backlogs are cleaned up, clear-edged systems are put in place, and front-end decision making is practiced. There's a palpable increase in cooperation and the quality of communications. All we've done is install better wiring and new spark plugs.

Nothing is so contagious as an example. We never do great good or great evil without bringing about more of the same on the part of others.

—FRANÇOIS DE LA ROCHEFOUCAULD

The system doesn't get rid of problems and challenges—it simply lets them be noticed much sooner and negotiated with more grace and ease.

By the way . . .

○ Where is the bottleneck in your personal workflow? What is the oldest communication not dealt with? What could you do to unstick it?

○ Which lists or structures that you use to manage yourself are not complete? How could you get them totally caught up?

○ Where is the bottleneck in your work groups (or family) in terms of things getting done? How could you improve it?

32.

The effectiveness of your system is inversely proportional to your awareness of it.

When you have to focus on your system, you are detouring energy that could be used to create and produce with your system. The objective of system installation, change, or enhancement is to get "system" off your mind again as soon as possible.

System Success: Silent Running

THE BETTER YOUR SYSTEMS, the more you don't know you have them. The less attention you pay to them, the more functional they probably are. The only time you will notice them is when they don't work or when you have to be too conscious about your use of them. You want to be working, doing, thinking, creating, and dealing with things—not focused on how you're doing them. You want to enjoy driving your car in the countryside without thinking about how to shift gears or work the climate control.

> *I must create a System, or be enslav'd by another Man's.*
>
> —WILLIAM BLAKE

Creating smoothly running silent systems is often the greatest improvement opportunity for enhanced productivity. Nine out of ten times, people have workflow systems that don't work, because they *are* too much work. Most of the organizing gear and software sold in the last twenty-five years makes sense conceptually but doesn't function as fast as what people are trying to coordinate.

When the amount of what has to be managed increases in speed and volume, a system will start to fall apart if its design is flawed or the habits of the operator are not grooved on "automatic."

An example of a poorly designed system is a reference filing system that stuffs multiple files into labeled hanging file holders. Volume and speed will kill it. There's often a mountain of information that ought to be in there but isn't. No one wants to put anything into overstuffed, complicated filing cabinets. Labeled files (not the hangers), with one file per folder (or even better without hangers), can withstand increased pressure without giving out. Another example of a systemic bottleneck is using the computer's mouse for things that speed keys can handle four times as fast. We often watch sophisticated professionals block their constructive thinking and communication process because it takes them too much conscious effort to bring up, address, write, and send e-mails.

The chains that bind us most closely are the ones that we have broken.

—ANTONIO PORCHIA

You must establish your own comfortable "grooved" workflow system. You need your own "home base," discretely yours, with all your work-processing tools and behaviors set on automatic. You don't want to have to retread your processing paths every time you try to sit down and get to work. I've been on the road 250 days a year for the last twenty years, and I can work reasonably well in a virtual work space. But I can work better in *my* office, with *my* desk, *my* files, and *my* tools all in place. Undisturbed. Because I like to be able to move with maximum efficiency—no resistance or residue.

By the way . . .

○ What procedures have you created that work because you no longer think about them—you just use them?

○ What parts of your systems do you have to keep thinking about? What could you do to get them more on "automatic"?

○ How is your work space at home? What could you do to ensure that you have a more functional life-management control room or cockpit?

33.

Function follows form.

In many ways, creating the right context and structure will ensure production and performance. The form will often trigger the focus that then fuels the intention, which produces creative energy and content. If you want to exercise, put on your exercise clothing. If you want to write a book, make up a title and boot your word processor. Want something at work to move forward? Pick the topic and set the meeting. Build it, and they will come.

Which Parts of Your Pot Need Stirring?

THIS ESSAY is about a level of application of our methodologies that, frankly, few people have yet tasted. And it's so immediately and easily available, with such potential value to the quality of your life, I am moved to remind you about it.

> *Throw your heart over the fence and the rest will follow.*
>
> —NORMAN VINCENT PEALE

What if you could rest assured that all the parts of your pot that need stirring are getting stirred? Let me explain. You have many levels of expression, interest, and focus in your life that can add tremendous richness and depth to your experience, in addition to the hundreds of basic things you have to be responsible for, day to day. That is, if you pay attention to them. Your kids, your network of friends, your love of cooking, your coin collection, and your golf swing. Your investments, your travel itch, your crazy thinking. Your favorite quotes, your personal affirmations, your penchant for Mozart, and your dreams of the future.

These, or dozens of similar things that hold some form of potential fascination and meaning for you, are out there right now, waiting for you to come to their table and play. All you have to do is engage, and you can do that in a few seconds. But if you're like me, you forget.

Man is not the creature of circumstances. Circumstances are the creatures of men.
—BENJAMIN DISRAELI

I forget to focus on my friends. I forget to think about giving random presents. I forget, believe it or not, about having fun. I forget about what constructive things I could do given my position with our office staff next week. I forget about a zillion things that would be way cool to do on a rainy Saturday afternoon. And, yes, I forget to dream.

So I put reminders in my personal-management system, and I see them in my weekly review. Few people I know really grasp the power of the basic weekly review. This is black-belt personal management for the twenty-first-century person: consistently clearing your head, identifying outcomes and actions, organizing and updating lists, to maintain a clear head and a proactive frame of mind. And even fewer have tasted beyond black belt (first-degree black belt is only the beginning!)—they haven't learned to work their creative *checklists*.

Life is a series of inspired follies. The difficulty is to find them to do. Never lose a chance: it doesn't come every day.
—GEORGE BERNARD SHAW

Get the habit of the weekly review. Then plug in to that review all the lists that might trigger a worthwhile thought that could add value to your life. Don't let things stick to the bottom of your pot.

By the way . . .

○ What areas of your life have you perhaps neglected more than you would like? How could you build in a reminder to think about them more consistently?

○ What meeting might you want to create, just to start something happening?

You can't win a game you haven't defined.

Games are fun only when you know very specifically what the goal is. The vision of "playing soccer" is realized only with a playing field and a goal at the end. And the activity of kicking the ball is most galvanized by knowing exactly where you want to kick it. The game of work requires the same edges and directions.

The Scary Swampland Between Thinking and Doing

PETER DRUCKER admonished that the greatest task of knowledge work was to "define your work." Well, I've discovered that the greatest challenges in defining your work are (1) to think about what you're doing and (2) to do something about what you're thinking.

The work will teach you how to do it.
—ESTONIAN PROVERB

Those behaviors don't come easily. People tend to get busy doing all kinds of activities, without clear operational targets, and they tend to think, fret, and talk a lot about all sorts of ideas and possibilities without grounding them into physical outcomes.

These two challenges come together in appropriately defining and managing a real and complete list of projects. I define a "project" as any outcome you've committed to that requires more than one action step to get there. To me, both "Get a new lamp for my desk" and "Buy the company" are projects. Given that definition, you probably have between thirty and a hundred projects right now. The problem is not that you have them all but that you probably don't know exactly what you have.

The ability to convert ideas to things is the secret of outward success.
—HENRY WARD BEECHER

People unconsciously resist creating a projects list, and yet it is the master key to maintaining relaxed control in life and work on a day-to-day basis. It's the cornerstone of the weekly review, which itself is the key activity I've found to manage the overwhelming possibilities of our focus.

On the one hand, some people are highly visionary and conceptual in their thinking about work. Their minds are filled with big initiatives, such as entering the European market, preventing burnout in the workplace, restructuring the senior team, or deepening a relationship with a client or strategic partner. They often have trouble understanding what we mean when we ask, "What project(s) do you have about that?" For them, the challenge is to decide what they need to make happen, in order to make those big things happen. When we coach these folks, we often have to start

When you're up to your ass in alligators, it's hard to remember that your purpose is draining the swamp.
—GEORGE NAPPER

up at the vision or "areas of focus" level and squeeze them down into the projects they need to define. They need to get "Change my corporate culture" down to "Research change-management consulting firms" and organize *that* on their projects list. But they resist it like the plague.

On the other hand, there are people who have tons of calls, e-mails, agendas with staff, meetings, and errands, but they haven't precisely clarified all the operational outcomes that are driving much of this activity, so they can't manage them effectively to completion. Coaching them often means going through all their next-action lists and capturing the projects that are creating them. Their phone slip "Call Bob Smith re: consulting proposal" should trigger "Research change-management consulting firms" on their projects list. But they, too, resist this like the plague.

Yet what relief when any of these people actually create such a list! A complete and accurately defined list of projects, kept current and reviewed on at least a weekly basis, is a master key to stress-free productivity. And it is still nonexistent for most people we encounter. Perhaps that's because it really works.

By the way . . .

○ Do you have a list of all your projects? When could you take a half hour and create it?

○ What situation has shown up in the last few days that you have committed to resolve or complete? Is that on your list?

35.

Whenever two or more are responsible for something, usually nobody is.

When the locus of focus for action is distributed, creative discomfort for progress is often dulled and perception of relevant details is blunted. Shared responsibility works only when at least one person assumes that he or she will be totally responsible. A boat has one skipper at a time.

The Inner Committee

SOMETIMES I GET MYSELF into trouble. As I participate in this game of life and work, I assume that my self-management team is really just one person. But, alas, I'm a committee.

Actually, I *have* a committee, but it often acts as if it's in charge. And I suffer the slings and arrows of outrageous fortune that befall committees. Each member of my internal committee parades righteousness when it's his or her turn to talk, and sometimes no one accepts responsibility for what happens (or doesn't happen) because of the lack of consensus or leadership. Parts of me get attracted to pursue all kinds of things that seem totally important in the moment I focus on them but (in the larger scheme of things) are amazingly irrelevant or downright detrimental to the welfare of the whole

If you had to identify, in one word, the reason why the human race has not achieved, and never will achieve, its full potential, that word would be: "meetings."

—DAVE BARRY

enterprise. And it's so easy to say (from any conveniently chosen perspective), "It wasn't *my* responsibility. *They* did it!"

Or to say, *"They didn't do it,"* which is more likely the case.

To get something done, a committee should consist of no more than three men, two of whom are absent.

—ROBERT
COPELAND

If I could just get my inner management committee into consensus—or shut it up—I'd probably never experience stress. Different perspectives and points of view can be valuable, but there's a problem when I give them equal reign and responsibility. The trouble comes when Part A says, "Do X," and Part B says, "Do Y." And then X happens, and Part B goes into rebellion. Or Y happens, and Part A feels abandoned and depressed.

"If everybody minded their own business," the Duchess said, in a hoarse growl, "the world would go round a great deal faster than it does."

—LEWIS CARROLL

Fortunately, there is a CEO. The challenge is to get him to show up at the table at the right time to take his appropriate role in high-level analysis, intelligent decision making, and assurance of appropriate implementation. When he abdicates those responsibilities, my company's in trouble.

"Appropriate implementation"—there's my strategic issue if ever there was one! If I could be assured that the not-so-smart (but highly energetic) part of me could be corralled and disciplined into doing the things or not doing the things that the intelligent part of me has concluded are the best choices for The Plan—wow! Heaven on earth. But getting the physical and material resources lined up and marching in the right direction, getting the things done that really need doing, consistently—that's the really big challenge.

One of the tricks I've learned and continually need to practice is setting up the appropriate organizational structure to leverage the strengths of each member of my committee. I need the right parts of me doing the right kinds of activities, given their job, and a system to keep that happening.

I don't need discipline. I need a disciplined approach. The creative, active, energetic part of me needs something to *do*, something that it *can* do and can *complete*—successfully, now. The intelligent, sensitive, aware part of me needs to be given an appropriate arena within which to support and express the higher vision and values that lie deeper within. I need to have

> *A committee can make a decision that is dumber than any of its members.*
> —DAVID COBLITZ

and to capture creative ideas with abandon. And I need to have the focused behaviors and systems required to translate them into next actions and physical reality. This is organization development, from the inside out.

By the way . . .
○ Who's the rebel on your inner committee?
○ What forum can you establish to ensure that your CEO is in charge?

36.

Prime your principles
instead of policing your policies.

Rules tend to show up because principles are not clear or trusted. When you know that people have bought into standards, you can give them freedom for decisions and behaviors. If this alignment doesn't exist, you must micromanage with regulations, expending much more energy in the long run.

You Are at Your Best When . . .

HOW ARE YOU DOING what you're doing, when you're doing it at your best? How is your work group doing what it's doing, when it's at its best? Or your board? Or your primary relationship?

People should know what you stand for. They should also know what you won't stand for.

—UNKNOWN

It's a great way to think about the real application of the noble advice of the pundits: "Focus on your values." Do this: Title a page *"We are at our best when . . ."* and keep writing as long as something shows up. Make sure it's the truth and said as well as you can say it. Then share it with whomever you ought to.

Lately I've been experiencing that kind of quality thinking about how I work, how I like to work, and how I want to work—my values, my principles, my standards. Last year, we began to add people to our team. On a long plane trip with my wife, prior to a meeting with the group, we went through that drill for ourselves. With only the two of us in our business, we hadn't needed to focus on our company standards that much. There were a lot of clear "givens" that underlay how we have lived and worked closely together over the last decade. No big deal. But now we had people joining our merry band. We didn't want to surprise them later with our priorities about how we operate—or vice versa.

Simple, clear purpose and principles give rise to complex and intelligent behavior. Complex rules and regulations give rise to simple and stupid behavior.

—DEE HOCK

I've experienced (more times than I like to admit) avoiding the slightly uncomfortable conversations with others I should have had on the front end and then endured much more excruciating ones on the back end. A great source of stress in personal and professional relationships is the mismatch of standards you aren't aware of when you make the initial agreements. Unfortunately, you usually recognize your own expectations of appropriate behavior only after they've been violated.

Not everything that can be counted counts, and not everything that counts can be counted.

—ALBERT EINSTEIN

Our new and expanding team in my company has spent the past few months becoming more conscious of defining and expressing our collective values. We've identified over twenty, but I'll share just a few:

○ We consistently challenge ourselves to play in the bigger game.
○ In our day-to-day interactions, we are directed by curiosity instead of control.
○ It is safe for all of us to explore, express, and move on.
○ We support creative, conscious risk taking.
○ We are respectfully nice.

As a group, we've challenged ourselves to keep these values alive and real. We've posed questions around each of them: Are we living up to this one? How aren't we? How could we do it better? An example of that would be . . . ?

"Company principles" can often be like "motherhood and apple pie," without much connection to the real, everyday world. Unless they really are yours.

By the way . . .

○ Have you created a checklist of your key principles to live and work by? With whom should you share it?

○ Who's driving you up the wall? Why? What standard do you hold that that person's behavior violates?

37.

Use your mind to think *about* your work, instead of thinking *of* it.

Your mind does not remember or remind very well, compared to what a good system can manage. What it does do well is review options and available information and then put together "how-tos." It's not free to do that if it's trying to remember and remind. Without an airtight system, it must work at a lower level than it should and becomes a misused resource.

Is Form Formless?

THERE'S SOMETHING about form that intrigues me. Before you have it, you waver. Once you have it, you transcend it. There's only before and after. You're never just form.

It is in self-limitation that a master first shows himself.

—JOHANN GOETHE

There is a form to driving a car. Before you have it, you are focused on how to do it. Once you know how to do it, you use it for getting somewhere, expressing yourself "on the open road," exploring, and socializing. You are never just driving a car.

In karate, I practiced "forms" or "katas." They are sets of stylized moves—very specific responses to two or more imaginary adversaries. Learning the forms takes intense concentration and discipline. Once you learn it, the form is the arena within which you continually sharpen focus, speed, and precision. You are never

*Once you accept
your own death, all
of a sudden you're
free to live. You no
longer care about
your reputation. You
no longer care except
so far as your life can
be used tactically—
to promote a cause
you believe in.*

—SAUL ALINSKY

just doing a kata. A black belt who gets jumped in a dark alley doesn't do "the form." It's never that pretty or clean. But he does what he does with focus, speed, and precision, which he could never have otherwise acquired.

There's a form to mastering work. You collect it, process it, organize it, and review it, choosing actions based upon an interplay with what you *can* do at the moment and what you want to accomplish or maintain (your "job"). Until you get the form, you'll be busy at the effect of your work. After you get it, you'll constantly be open to expanding awareness and expression of what your "work" really is.

Form. You can't do, without it. Until you do, without it.

By the way . . .

○ What are you still asking your mind to remind you about? How could you relieve it of that job?

○ What discipline or structure do you need to complete or install, if any, to free yourself for your higher-level thinking?

38.

You are thinking more valuably than you may think.

Many of the ideas that you have, if not immediately and obviously valuable in the moment, contain the germ of something that may be extremely useful. You simply may not see it yet. Give yourself the freedom to capture all kinds of thoughts that you can later reassess. Make freeform note taking a habit, whenever you are getting input from other sources—meetings, conversations, voice mail—or when you're just brainstorming with yourself. Make a clear distinction between collecting, processing, and organizing, and give yourself permission to collect anything without censure or analysis. The psychologists call this "distributed cognition." It will add a major creative source to your work and your life.

Freedom and Form Fun

MUCH OF WHAT I've uncovered about productivity and the use of personal gear seems to have a cosmic rhythm to it. It's been a strange meeting place for me of the sublime and the mundane. The reason I've grown to love my in-basket so much is not just a kinky fetish for stacking plastic trays; it's that I get to ex-

> *No great invention started with a business plan.*
> —UNKNOWN

press, create, and capture things with great freedom and then "bring it all home" into coherence as I process them. One allows the other.

The reason I love my easy-flowing, great-feeling, ballpoint or felt-tipped pen and a nice clean legal pad to write all over is the spontaneity they foster in my messy brainstorming, planning, and note taking. I trust that the ideas will get digested and assessed for value that I don't yet see.

The primary tools that one needs in modern day culture are to know how to make things up, and how to figure things out. This is creativity in two of its forms. These are called imagination and problem-solving.
—STEVEN SNYDER

I love the high-tech/high-touch dance of handwriting notes and then assimilating and processing them into the computer. I often coach people who are looking for the perfect way to use only one or the other—all paper or all computer. I've found that doing both increases the use and value of both. I love the fact that I've thrown away thousands of things I've written on hotel notepads, for the few that stood the test of later scrutiny (and that's not always because of last night's wine!).

The best way to get a good idea is to get lots of ideas.
—LINUS PAULING

My life and work seem to have that same kind of rhythm, but on a bigger scale. I go through cycles of six to twelve months when I'm coming up with new projects and things to do like crazy. My lists are like my plum trees in summer, when they're so full of ripe fruit we have to run out every day to catch what's falling. Then I spend the next six to twelve months working to finish up, handle, and follow through on stuff to get back some measure of control.

The "silly" question is the first intimation of some totally new development.
—ALFRED NORTH WHITEHEAD

Expansion and contraction. Creation and completion. Right brain, left brain. Yin and yang. The more we bring these polarities into balance, the more productive we are. Make sure you're giving yourself permission to have the tools you want to support this process.

And add to this the more subtle interaction—you uncover order as you expand. You unlock the infinite as you limit with discipline. Ask a good gardener. Express with freedom, and direction will emerge. Resolve with focus, and creativity will bloom.

Engaging, isn't it?

By the way . . .

○ What could you brainstorm on right now? How about having an idea you've not had before?

○ Where and when are you most likely to get random but potentially useful thoughts? Do you have an easy place to capture them?

○ What's your favorite writing tool? Where is it? How could you make it more ubiquitously accessible?

39.

The necessity to plan and organize is inversely proportional to your perceived resources.

If you have all the time, money, and energy in the world, why bother managing them? Just wander around and let things show up, or just acquire things as you think of them. It's only when you have the hard choices about how to allocate limited resources that the real need for clarity of direction and efficiency emerges. The most "lean and mean" (and creative) companies will be the ones with the greatest gap between their vision and their current reality. The most effective people will be the ones who have the least, relative to what they have committed to.

Why the Human Race Is Taking So Long to Evolve

I HAVE DISCOVERED why humanity is not a whole lot better off than it is, after all this time. What we truly most need to do is often what we most feel like avoiding.

God forgives those who invent what they need.

—LILLIAN HELLMAN

Frequently, the last thing in the world we are inclined to do is exactly what would most improve the situation. When you most need to plan is usually when you think you don't have time to plan. When you most need to get organized is when you least feel you can afford to stop and do it. When you are depressed, happy people are the most disturbing to you.

Just think of it. What if, every time you started to go into too much debt, you felt like saving money? What if, every time you felt stressed about a project or situation, you got an uncontrollable urge to stop everything, go into a conference room with two other key people for an hour, and regroup about the focus and the tactics and the next actions about it? What if, every time you began to lose your temper, you felt compelled to take a breath, balance yourself emotionally, and shift your perspective to a more positive viewpoint? What if, every time things got overwhelming, the thing you most felt like doing was cleaning up all the open loops in your life and reviewing and renegotiating all your commitments at the multiple levels on which you operate? If we all acted this way, we would have created a utopian golden age long ago.

Whenever I am rested and feeling good, I can't help feeling frivolous.

—MARK TWAIN

The basic difference between an ordinary man and a warrior is that a warrior takes everything as a challenge while an ordinary man takes everything either as a blessing or a curse.

—CARLOS CASTANEDA

What compounds the sluggishness of our evolutionary crawl is that when we actually *do* have the time, *are* in a better mood, *have* more of a sense of control, we don't feel enough pressure to compel us to do what we know we should be doing to prevent the nasty negative situations from showing up *again*. When the heat's on, we tell ourselves we'll get organized—later. We'll be nicer to ourselves and other people—later. We'll be more strategic and proactive—later.

The most gifted members of the human species are at their creative best when they cannot have their way, and must compensate for what they miss by realizing and cultivating their capacities and talents.

—ERIC HOFFER

Later comes, and the heat's off. "If I had more money, then I'd really be a lot more creative." Really? "If I just had more time, I'd really . . . (fill in the blank)." Are you sure? If we had more time and money, we'd likely feel even *less* like doing what we think we should feel like doing. Under stress, we'll default to habits and not do what we need to do. When things relax, we

Change and growth take place when a person has risked himself and dares to become involved with experimenting with his own life.

—HERBERT OTTO

won't feel the need to go to work to change the habits—as sure as gravity.

Unless we do the exceptional. Unless we break free of the confines of earthly limitations and access something that lifts us above this vale of tears. Unless we defy gravity. And we will, sooner or later. The point is, the world isn't designed to evolve—we are.

By the way . . .

○ What is the biggest thing you have accomplished, with the least amount of initial resources?

○ What potential future crisis ought you be dealing with, now?

○ What is the project or commitment you currently have, for which you feel you have the least resources to get it done? What constructive thinking could you apply to it, and when?

PART IV

RELAX AND GET IN MOTION

or

How to Be Where the Action Is

Sometimes the old homespun admonition, "Just *do* it!" seems called for. The problem is, *what* to do is often not immediately self-evident. Our minds, unchecked, can create a paralyzing fog of righteous worry—we're too smart to start. But we can harness our mental horsepower to trigger forward motion and transform pressure into easy productivity. Knowing how to get into the swing of things, on call, is a subtle and masterful craft.

40.

You're the only one playing your game.

You have created, accepted, or promoted whatever you are experiencing. That's the great news, because you're in charge and you can change it if you want. You are your own writer, producer, director, and yet merely an extra in everyone else's play. The best teams know and expect that integrity of the players. The best players manage their own game no matter what. We're all alone in this together.

The New Fundamentals

FROM TIME TO TIME, human resource directors have asked me to submit proposals describing how what I teach fits in with their management and professional-development curriculum. Each and every time I've studied their programs and failed to find a slot into which it fits. It's not that their criteria for effectiveness are wrong. It's that there's something that's still missing underlying the much-sought-after qualities of leadership, results focus, communication, creativity, planning, and the like. There are important qualities that to a large extent have not yet been recognized as critical behaviors for knowledge work.

What about the ability to . . .

> *When trouble arises and things look bad, there is always one individual who perceives a solution and is willing to take command. Very often, that individual is crazy.*
>
> —DAVE BARRY

○ maintain relaxed control amid overwhelming amounts of incoming stuff,

○ define doable projects from ambiguous direction, initiatives, and pressures,

○ decide actions required when things show up versus when they blow up,

○ regroup, recalibrate priorities, and regain balance rapidly with new information and changing circumstances,

○ be alone, in cooperation with everyone else,

○ renegotiate implicit and explicit agreements with themselves and others,

○ express and consider any ideas, including bad ones, in front of their staff and then evaluate them objectively,

○ refocus rapidly on desired outcomes and next actions when confronted with challenging obstacles, and

○ consistently capture, clarify, update, review, reassess, and renegotiate their life and work commitments, so personal energies are fully available for the job at hand?

> *This responsibility for thinking through what one's contribution should be and one's own responsibility as a knowledge worker rests on each individual. In the knowledge organization it becomes everybody's responsibility, regardless of his or her particular job.*
>
> —PETER F. DRUCKER

Am I missing something here? Why have I seldom seen these criteria formally used for an evaluation of the skills or performance of professionals? Would you want to hire or work for someone who didn't score well on any of these? If someone can't direct and manage him- or herself amid intense input and rapidly changing landscapes, how on earth could he or she be expected to lead or manage anyone else?

I contend that a competitive edge, personal and organizational, is maintained by one's ability to deal with surprise. It's when the pressures of unexpected change challenge the systems and behaviors that excellence is really demonstrated.

Change has always created disruption and discomfort. What's new is how often that's happening. Is "Readiness for Anything" on your performance reviews yet?

By the way . . .

○ Is there a situation you wish were different but that you assume you can do nothing about? What next action *could* you take, if you were willing to do so? Where and when can you do it?

○ Who are the most productive people you know? Would you consider them low or high maintenance?

41.

Too controlled is out of control.

In golf and tennis, too firm a grip can cause you to "choke" a shot. Hanging on too tightly can limit your ability to deal with things from the most productive perspective. Micromanaging—getting too wrapped around the axles of life and work—can be a seductive trap in getting things done. Fine points are fine, as long as there's a point.

Are You an "Organizing Groupie"?

I'VE BECOME MORE AWARE lately of "organizing groupies"—people who dedicate an inordinate amount of time and energy to experimenting with organizing details that don't seem to me nearly worth the effort. This might sound strange coming from someone who's spent years researching the best practices of personal and interactive productivity. To be sure, I've spent countless hours exploring systems, software, gear, and techniques in order to find out the absolute best ways to get something done with the least amount of work. And much of that time was spent running down rabbit trails that proved to be wrong turns. The difference may be that I've focused on achieving the specific results of getting things off my mind and making things happen easily—not with simply "getting organized."

So what's the distinction? Just "getting organized" misses the crucial point: the need for thinking and intuitive decision making to get real work done. Once people catch on to the power of organization per se, they sometimes go too far and try to microorganize everything: "Let's create a system so you won't have to think at all!" But it can't be done. My systems do indeed relieve the mind of the tasks of remembering and reminding as much as I can, but they don't replace the need for regular executive thinking about my stuff. Organizing systems are there purely to serve as crude placeholders for targets and their critical parts and pieces. You must still engage your mind, your intelligence, and your vision to integrate those moving parts into the whole of how you interact with your world. No matter how good you are at

Some people have nothing very well organized. And some people have nothing, very well organized.
—UNKNOWN

If everything's under control, you're going too slow.
—MARIO ANDRETTI

creating macros in your spreadsheet or how sophisticated your PDA add-on, you won't be able to push a button, run a formula, and have the result be "Call Fred." Even if it did, you would have to consider a lot more things not on the spreadsheet or in your PDA to trust that judgment about your action decision.

Countless questions have been e-mailed to me asking for the best ways and tools to organize project thinking. People want to know how to relate project pieces to each other and to all the other projects and their pieces. Ninety-nine percent of the time, my answer is the same: "Once a week, do a thorough review of all your projects in as much detail as you need to. If you do, your systems will work. If you don't, no system will work." This kind of weekly conscious overviewing of projects and their associated actions keeps you organized with incredible effectiveness, because it's really about capturing, catalyzing, and executing creative thinking, not about "getting organized."

The passion for a certain quality of experience (relaxation, fun, productive in-your-zone-ness) or the desire to have something show up that you really want (a painting, a poem, a new company, a successful product launch) can generate high motivation for getting organized in order to get there. But don't let enthrallment with your form (organization) detract from your function (outcome).

By the way . . .

○ Is there any "overkill" in your system? What tools or procedures have you set up that you are not using? What can be eliminated?

○ Do you feel you need to do more "project management"? Are you examining appropriate details and status of all your projects completely and consistently enough? If not, what could you do to install a more regular review process?

42.

The better you get,
the better you'd better get.

As you open your flow, as you produce more value with less effort, it graduates your responsibilities and your attraction to bigger problems and opportunities—automatically. Hang on. Increasing your effectiveness is not the easy path, though it is by far the most rewarding.

Jump!

EVERY DECISION we make about what action to take at any time is an intuitive risk. I have twenty minutes before my next meeting— should I call Bob, work on Chapter 8, or get Susan's opinion on the new software?

The oversimplicity of ABC priorities or daily to-do lists can never really answer that question for any of us. No matter how organized we get, how squeaky-clean our systems and process are,

Howcum little kids practice, and big kids don't?
—STEVE SHULL

or how current our strategic and tactical planning is, we ultimately have to trust our hunches about the best thing for us to do at 10:43 A.M. or 3:22 P.M. today.

The vast majority of the coaching and training that I do installs a thought process and a good system for clearing the psychic decks, while framing perspective at the appropriate horizons to make good decisions. It never ultimately answers the question "What's the best thing for me to do right now?"

People would often love to be able to give up the nonstop responsibility for their intuitive judgment calls about the moment-to-moment allocation of their resources. That's why the ABC-priority or daily-to-do-list structures have seemed so attractive as a way to "get a grip." But reality has a way of demanding us to be more on our toes than that. As we mature in our life and work experience, the complexities, variables, and subtleties increase enormously. Simple answers are, for the most part, too simplistic.

You have to leave the city of your comfort and go into the wilderness of your intuition. What you'll discover will be wonderful. What you'll discover will be yourself.

—ALAN ALDA

So how can we really know for sure what action to take next? Prepare for the worst, imagine the best, and shoot down the middle. "Prepare for the worst" means to tie up all the loose ends and don't leave yourself vulnerable to the self-deflation of unclear and unrenegotiated commitments. "Imagine the best" means to keep focused on the most positive outcomes and energies you can. "Shoot down the middle" means jump.

A "mind like water" methodology doesn't replace the need for an intelligent, conscious you, in the moment. It simply allows you to make your intuitive leaps from a solid platform of trust instead of a slippery footing of hope.

By the way . . .

○ Are you finding it easier, or harder, to make important decisions in your life and work? Is there anything to learn from that?

○ What intuitive risk do you think you ought to take now? What's the worst that could happen if you took it? The best?

○ Do you have more regrets over the things you haven't done in life or the things you have?

43.

Trusting your action choice requires multilevel self-management.

Having clear, long-term goals can be insufficient to maximize your focus of energy in the details of life and work. And pristine organization of your details does not ensure truly productive activity. The appropriate use of an ad hoc five-minute window to take a short action to prevent a future annoyance can be as elegant an executive task as walking away from a chaotic morning's in-basket to think about how to move forward on your strategic objectives.

It's 9:45 in the Morning. What Should I Do?

WHAT'S THE BEST THING to do, right now, at this moment? I'm still working on how to get the best answer to that question. Frankly, I think anyone who tries to give you a simple formula for it is trying to sell you something. Many complex variables factor into that decision, in every instance, but the ultimate answer is this: Trust your intuition. And anyone who tells you there's a simple answer about how to access, understand, and analyze potentially accurate intuitive information is also trying to sell you something.

For knowledge workers, at least three sets of dynamics come into play about deciding what we do, and somewhat in this order:

An idealist believes the short run doesn't count. A cynic believes the long run doesn't matter. A realist believes that what is done or left undone in the short run determines the long run.
—SYDNEY J. HARRIS

1. Context (What *can* I do at this moment?)
2. Type of work (Do I do what I've already defined needs doing, do new work that I didn't expect as it shows up, or process my stuff to update my inventory of what needs doing?)
3. Level of work (Should I be focusing on an e-mail I need to answer, a project I need to complete, an area of responsibility I need to do something about, a goal or objective I need to move on, or a destiny I need to fulfill?)

Trifles make perfection, and perfection is no trifle.
—MICHELANGELO

Ignore any one of these three frameworks at your peril. Improve your management of any one of them, and you'll enjoy an energy rush.

1. Context: If you're surprised with an extra fifteen minutes before a delayed meeting at an office on another floor of your building, do you have already at hand all the calls you need to make on all the open loops in your life? If not, you'll tend to be reactive instead of proactive, and internal pressure on yourself will likely mount. If you do have that list and you trust it has all the calls you need to make, you can more easily function in your "zone."
2. Doing work and defining work to do: If you don't want to deal with five hundred e-mails, figuring out what they mean and what you need to do about them, you'll be sucked into the most immediate pull on your energy from your office and your environment. Your actions will probably then spring from avoidance instead of engagement. If you tackle and dispatch them, because you sense you really need to "clear the decks" to free up your attention for something else, you'll be on a roll.
3. Multiple horizons of commitment: And if you haven't had the appropriate discussions with your boss, your spouse, or your partner that you know you need to, given the changes in your life and career to which you feel you must pay attention, you'll be in some level of contraction instead of expansion—professionally, psychologically, or spiritually. If you've truly managed

those levels of conversation with yourself and others appropriately, you'll enjoy an energetic and balanced focus.

You exist on many levels. If you're avoiding any of them, you may be short-sheeting all of them. To the degree you accept the responsibility for managing them equally, you'll find it easier to enjoy and transcend the whole game.

It is easy to dodge our responsibilities, but we cannot dodge the consequences of dodging our responsibilities.
—E. C. MCKENZIE

By the way . . .

○ What would you do today at work if you found yourself with thirty free minutes? Are you prepared in case this opportunity arises?

○ What conversations, at what horizon, are due or overdue for you?

44.

Your power is proportional to your ability to relax.

Speed and precision are the key ingredients to effective motion in the martial arts, and being relaxed allows for maximum control and focus. Might this be true anywhere else? You don't break boards or bricks with the greatest efficiency if you're uptight. Or handle four people who jump you in a dark alley. Or negotiate a deal. Or have the most appropriately deep and meaningful and risky conversation with your partner, your spouse, or your son. You'd better be relaxed. Find out what's stressing you, and deal with it—now—if you want to be truly effective on all levels at once. Being relaxed and capable of focusing on what's at hand, when it's at hand, without over- or underreacting, is a master skill. It's the context for accessing the greatest power.

The Freedom/Productivity Equation

I'VE READ THAT the history of productivity is the history of personal freedom. The context for this remark was that the degree of individual liberty in a society correlated with higher output per person or effort. That seems intuitively correct, though I'm not an expert in the history of work. What struck me was the truth of this within our own consciousness. The freer we are in our heads, the more creative output we can experience and

> *To the mind that is still, the whole universe surrenders.*
> —LIEH-TZU

deliver. But what if we're constricted in our heads? How do we create freedom there?

Most people actually have a lot of thinking going on about a lot of stuff in their life and work—stuff that is basically unproductive, distracting, and a source of unnecessary stress. This is at least a constraint, if not downright enslaving. Why is this happening? Is our brain just a tyrant controlling and punishing us? No, it's a wonderful servant, but not particularly intelligent, trying frantically to fulfill obligations laid on it by our internal commitments and agreements with others and ourselves. It's like a little kid constantly whining and pleading with us, "Don't forget—we've got to do something about this! We've got something to do, and we haven't figured it out yet!" Et cetera ad nauseam . . .

A useful definition of liberty is obtained only by seeking the principle of liberty in the main business of human life; that is to say, in the process by which men educate their responses and learn to control their environment.

—WALTER LIPPMANN

Unfortunately, that part of our psyche has no sense of past or future, so it operates as if everything should be getting done right now, all at once. It yanks our chain about this at any time, but usually not when we could actually do anything productive. It reminds us about the batteries after they've gone dead, not when we're standing in front of them at the store.

The really intelligent part of us (it's quite different from the chattering mind) can take control at the appropriate time. It can recognize its agreements and open loops in life and work, decide what's needed to complete them, and renegotiate all those options with itself elegantly. It knows it can do only one thing at a time and accepts what it's okay not to be doing. It can create the context for true mental freedom. It just can't assume full control of a situation, unless it can manage all those outcomes and actions in some external, objective, reviewable system.

In my seminars, I sometimes get pushback from people who look at my lists and systems and then say, "Gee, if I had to do all that thinking and tracking, it wouldn't make me more productive—it would be a waste of time!" I understand their reaction. Most of the systems that people have tried are incomplete or unclear in terms of outcomes desired and next actions required. People using those partial systems never got to the point of real freedom. So why bother? I wouldn't either.

But if you really pay attention to your mind's concerns and how to handle them (decide outcomes and take next-action steps, with reminders in a total and trusted system that's reviewed appropriately), you will be motivated to make the investment. And you will get the higher productivity that naturally comes from the increase in personal freedom.

By the way . . .

○ When have you recently felt the freest? How did you create that? How could you create more of that experience?

○ When have you felt the most effective? How did that relate to your ability to concentrate?

○ What is causing the most background noise in your life? How could you get it quiet?

45.

Surprises, expected, are no surprise.

When you plan that your plans may be interrupted or disturbed, you gain steadiness. Denial of the reality of constant change produces resistance and frustration. Complaining about interference creates a swampy backwater of unproductive energy. Eliminate the cause of the disruption, or accept and integrate it as part of your work—then get on with it.

Productively Peering into the Pit

POSITIVE THINKING is a tricky business. Once you are consciously aware of the creative power of your imagination, focusing purely on successful pictures and outcomes seems the only way to go. But to live a life of the best, there are times you must assume the worst.

Many self-awareness therapies and educational seminars spend at least some time unearthing "negative" events and memories from the past. As I became familiar with the principles of forward visioning, however, I questioned the need to do that. "Why delve into anything that's not what you want?" I asked myself. Then I discovered why. If I'm subliminally afraid of an experience or harbor judgments about it, it will hold me captive at some level. I will find myself uncon-

The pessimist complains about the wind; the optimist expects it to change; the realist adjusts the sails.

—WILLIAM ARTHUR WARD

sciously drawing the same or similar experiences toward me again. To get past them I must accept, acknowledge, forgive, and release my own negativity to be really free to direct all parts of me toward what I want.

Often I have found the one thing that can save is the thing which appears most to threaten. One has to go down into what one most fears and in the process . . . comes a saving flicker of light and energy that, even if it does not produce the courage of a hero, at any rate enables a trembling mortal to take one step further.

—LAURENS
VAN DER POST

Courage is not the absence of fear, but rather the judgment that something else is more important than fear.

—AMBROSE
REDMOON

If that sounds too personal-growth-ish to you, consider the positive application of that principle in the business world. A good management or project team at some point should address the question "What could go wrong, and could we handle it?" Is that naysaying and unproductive, negative thinking? Not at all. It's necessary, not only to build in intelligent contingencies but, more important, to face the worst head-on and deal with it conceptually and psychologically. Soldiers who address the possibility of death are much more likely to face the enemy effectively. They don't eliminate fear but transcend it to defuse its paralyzing effect.

Negative thinking—dwelling on the undesirable in fear or frustration—produces contraction. But directly addressing the possibility of not-so-ideal circumstances and integrating the experience into your forward motion build awareness and power. What you resist, you are stuck with. What you fear comes upon you. Trying to avoid or deny how "bad" it has been or could be, under the guise of "positive thinking," creates vulnerability for that event to blindside you. And the angst about the possibility of calamity will hold you hostage at an unconscious level, preventing the risk taking necessary for your expansion and success.

Maintaining a consistent intention of uplifting thoughts toward positive outcomes is not for the faint of heart. You must be willing to confront the whole gamut of historical and future potential realities, accept them for what they are (and are not), and keep moving toward what you want. That truly defuses the demons.

Life is what happens to you while you are making other plans.
—JOHN LENNON

How bad could it be? Could you handle it? Then you probably won't have to.

By the way . . .

○ Is there a downside possibility you ought to be examining in your life or work? Is there any contingency thinking that would serve you right now? What's the next step to do that?

○ What are you most afraid of losing? Is the fear holding you hostage about getting what you want?

46.

The longer your horizon, the smoother your moves.

People with the most elevated view of what they are doing perform the most elegant-looking actions. In one sense, the farther away the "there" is that you have targeted, the more options you can see about how to get there and the more relaxed and easy the course corrections are. Beginning drivers seem to make a lot of jerky movements with the wheel. Actually, they're making smooth movements to very short horizons.

The Rhythm of Things

I'VE BEEN THINKING a lot lately about the rhythm of things. I've been more aware of the cycles that we set up and how convenient it is to establish and maintain the rhythms. Weekly staff meetings, afternoon walks in the garden, the morning paper, annual strategic plans, annual holidays and retreats, daily meditations, and so on. The things I always do in my job, the people I always connect with regularly, and the restaurants I always choose. And how often I write essays.

How nice when we can create grooved-in behaviors that benefit us. We don't want to think about creating context; we just want to be *in* our contexts and reap the automatic rewards. Until, however, those rewards diminish, relative to the energy invested. That's when we enter into tricky territory. Too many times, we don't recognize when reality has shifted but we haven't, in our forms and behaviors. We keep doing what we've been doing, but the thrill is gone.

Something is different, and, more often than not, we don't immediately know what it is. Our old friends are not whom we really want to hang out with anymore. Our regular meetings are poorly attended, and we hate having to go, when there are other things that seem more important. Our favorite restaurant doesn't seem so favorite anymore. Our annual New Year's bash is just another thing we have to do.

When these forms reach a certain level of ossification, we will begin to feel a pressure internally, procrastinating about doing things that we used to do with enthusiasm. Because it was such a good idea to start with and because we got used to a positive benefit from it, we now think that we're getting lazy, old, or simply bored.

> *It is simplicity of intention that gives consistency to life.*
> —WILLIAM BRAITHWAITE

It could be any of those. Or it *could* be that the spirit of the situation is in charge and the forms must keep on morphing into something more vital and organic, for the highest good of the work really to be done. Your inner guidance mechanism may be letting you know that it's time to move on. You may be procrastinating and starting to goof off—or perhaps you're intuiting a change that needs to occur to continue to "follow the bouncing ball."

Are you willing to accept that there may be a bigger reality asserting itself through you and that you need to swallow hard and trust that giving up habitual rituals that have made a place in your comfort zone must now be sacrificed? What are you doing regularly now that you're not so inspired about? Or at least not nearly as much as when you first set it up and looked forward to it? Are you willing to look honestly at why you're doing it and be open to the next round of manifestation of your expression, which may mean giving up the old tried-and-true?

Things that turn us on are alive, vital, moving, growing, and changing in the forms and expressions that are connected to them.

We feel the energy and then create the rhythmic expressions of it at the time. But if we are to stay conscious, we must keep galloping lethargy at bay and risk losing what was once a good thing, to stay on course.

We act as though comfort and luxury were the chief requirements of life, when all we need to make us happy is something to be enthusiastic about.

—CHARLES KINGSLEY

A good friend of mine says, "There is no rest for the wicked, and the righteous don't need it." Another way to frame that might be this: When you stay attuned to where the real action is, you'll probably have to give up what used to work for something new that you're still not sure will work—and you've got to give it a shot. The "wicked" ones wait too long to sacrifice, recalibrate, and re-create the next form. The company goes belly up, the organization loses its members, and the flames are allowed to go out. You slave away to give a party, and nobody comes. The "righteous" are comfortable with creative discomfort. They get uncomfortable with the lack of the spark, the juice, and the flow. They follow their intuition, learning how to recognize what it is and when it speaks.

The best at this can tolerate that scary, awkward, vulnerable feeling of being out of step with their lover on the dance floor. They can admit things aren't working and restart. Now, that's romantic.

By the way . . .

○ What magazines should you cancel? Which new ones should you read?

○ What other things are you still doing even though you know the "thrill is gone"? What might you do instead?

○ If you really focused on the bigger picture for yourself, what new activities might you find engaging?

○ When's the last time you did something really unusual for you? Time to do another?

47.

You speed up by slowing down.

There is seldom enough time and energy to do what you want to do, when you focus only from the level of physical doing. You must constantly let go, relax, and refocus. If you're in a hurry, your vision can become myopic and your energy can be prematurely exhausted. With your clear intention inserted into the universe, trust that the method and the process and the resources for its manifestation will unfold in the grander scheme, in the best timing. Chill a bit, and allow yourself to play your bigger game.

Should the Pot Simmer?

YEARS AGO, when I was training in karate, I would find myself reaching plateaus where, no matter how hard and consistently I worked out, I didn't appear to be getting much better. This was highly frustrating, because I could easily remember when, with much less effort, I was able to reach new heights and results. Why was I working so hard and not seeming to get anywhere? Maybe I just needed to work harder!

> *Muddy water let stand will clear.*
> —CHINESE PROVERB

Then my coach would have me stop—totally. Quit working out. Become a vegetable. Not do anything for days, sometimes even weeks.

Then came reentry. Always mind-blowing. Cooler, classier, smoother, somehow at a new rhythm, from a new level, with subtle but critical improvement in my style, my finesse, my timing, my focus, my power. Wow.

Nothing can be more useful to a man than a determination not to be hurried.

—HENRY DAVID THOREAU

We learn, create, and grow on many levels, the conscious one being perhaps the least profound. Maybe our conscious focus is the chef, who directs the show. But the simmering, fabulous, complex chemistry that happens inside the pot—ah, that's the mystery.

For fast-acting relief, try slowing down.

—LILY TOMLIN

Trust your process. Trust the unseen formula that is working itself out through you, creating resolution and closure in ways beyond what you think you can do. Timing is everything. Don't push yours, or you may lose it.

Be patient. Patience is also preparation. It is the action before the act.

—NOAH BEN SHEA

What do you not have time to do—something that might feel like a waste of time—but you know that it's time to do? Walk in the garden? Have dinner with a friend? Take your team off site just to hang out together? Play laser guns with your kids? Walk away from the canvas, until you can't help taking up the brush again?

Relax. You have to put in the clutch to shift gears. You have to let go to reengage at another, more high-leveraged ratio. When you least feel like slowing down may be the most critical time to do it.

By the way . . .

○ What can you do today that you know you don't have time for?

○ What wheels seem to be spinning in your life and work that could use a rest?

○ When's the last time you did absolutely nothing?

48.

You don't have time to do any project.

You don't have time to do any project, because you actually can't do a project—you can do only action steps. Do enough of the appropriate actions, over time, and you make the world resemble the image you've committed to in your mind—taxes are done, the company is sold, the birthday party for Susan happens. But you didn't do those outcomes. They just showed up after you did lots of little physical, visible actions that made the world match your picture. That's "doing a project." Because people often don't translate it into next steps, the perception of lack of time to get a project done prevents any motion at all. Many a mission-critical project is hung up right now that has a next action that could be done in less than two minutes, were it identified.

The Subtle Sirens of the "Long Term"

ARE YOU AVOIDING action right now on "long-term projects," because they are "long-term projects"?

In our coaching work with senior-level professionals and executives, we often uncover projects and goals that have been labeled "long term." Things like "restructure the department," "create a strategic task force," and "develop a personal-investment strategy." When I ask, "What's the next action on that?" more often than not, they haven't figured one out. And, somewhat sheepishly and defensively, they excuse their lack of an action step with the comment, "Well, that's really a long-term project . . ."!

The distance is nothing; it's only the first step that is difficult.

—MADAME DU DEFFAND

The great French marshal Lyautey once asked his gardener to plant a tree. The gardener objected that the tree was slow growing and would not reach maturity for one hundred years. The marshal replied, "In that case, there is no time to lose; plant it this afternoon!

—JOHN F. KENNEDY

There's a subtle but critical difference between something that is long term and something in the category of "someday/maybe." Either a project is an open loop to close, as soon as possible, or it is not. "As soon as possible" may be seven years, but it is still "as soon as possible." And if it's an open loop to close, there is a next action on it that must be determined before any progress will take place. "As soon as possible" turns into "never" unless next physical visible-action steps are determined.

And no matter how far away a goal may be, there is something that can be done toward it immediately, if you're sincere about it. "Land on Mars" as a project still comes down to something like "Call Fred about the Mars budget proposal" that can be accomplished as soon and as easily as any other activity in our inventory of work at hand.

One of the best ways to procrastinate and deflate real motivation is to create big goals that are interpreted as "long term." As soon as we set those goals or identify those kinds of projects, we tend to feel smug and self-congratulatory and pseudocomplete about them, just because we've "committed to them," and our drive to close the loop starts to fizzle. Short-term deliverables about the long-term goals are a critical motivating factor, and real next actions that we can actually do within the next few hours or days galvanize the inspiration.

It's absolutely fine to put something on your "someday/maybe" list (I currently have over a hundred projects on mine). Just be honest with yourself about whether it should be on that list or on your real projects list. If it's a real project, long term or not, it has to have a next action for you to be at peace with yourself. If you haven't figured one out, it's a "someday/maybe" project by default.

"Long term" just means that "as soon as possible" will take more next actions.

By the way . . .

○ What's the longest-term project or goal you've actually committed to? Is there an action step determined?

○ What's a project you'd love to do but "don't have time" for? If you were to move on it, what's the next action?

49.

Small things, done consistently, create major impact.

*Real change occurs not with a flash in the pan but with steady
engagement at some new level of interaction. An automatic investment
of a small percentage of your income, attending an exercise class every
week, consistently sharing about your realities with your staff or family,
sitting down to a regular contemplative or meditative reflection every
evening—these are the keys to significant progress.*

The Critical 20 Percent

A SENIOR AND very sophisticated executive client of ours recently
gave us some interesting feedback about our workflow methods.

He said, "Your stuff impacts at the critical twenty-
percent level. Nobody will even try to absorb and
manage two hundred percent of what they can
do. But they will take on enough to let themselves
get ten percent behind their curve. And when you
are ten percent behind, you feel like crap. But, on
the other hand, if you can manage to get ten percent ahead, you're transformed and on top of
your world. That's only at the most a twenty-percent factor. But to
go from one to the other is a quantum leap. Your stuff is so simple
and so basic, but the profundity lies in its ability to make that kind
of difference."

*He who can take no
interest in what is
small will take false
interest in what is
great.*

—JOHN RUSKIN

I'd never quite thought of it that way, but it's true. It's also a very useful way to frame the value of defining projects, deciding actions, and managing them with integrity and thoroughness. It's not about new skills or new behaviors. It's about instigating those behaviors on the front end instead of the back and taking charge of the mundane aspects of life and work as they show up.

The difference between surfing your wave and feeling pummeled by it is huge. But what makes that difference is probably much less than you think.

What's tricky is that it takes an equally small amount of consistent *negative* behaviors to create significant unwanted consequences. Habitual self-degrading self-talk, though seemingly minor in the moment, reinforces lowered self-esteem and performance overall. Little stuff, unchecked, can create some of the worst problems.

Either way, the small actions we engage in regularly are the linchpins to the major results we experience.

In the end, it is attention to detail that makes all the difference. It's the center fielder's extra two steps to the left, the salesman's memory for names, the lover's phone call, the soldier's clean weapon. It is the thing that separates the winners from the losers, the men from the boys and, very often, the living from the dead.

—DAVID NOONAN

By the way . . .

○ Bring to mind one significant, permanent, positive change that has happened in your life. What small things were you doing consistently that created and/or allowed it to happen?

○ Right now what one small thing, if installed as a regular activity, would potentially have an enormous payoff for you?

50.

You have to do something to know something.

The development of real knowledge requires intentional activity. If you wait to know something before you do something, likely neither will happen. As you faithfully move your body, your thinking, and your spirit, things will unfold that would be inaccessible in any other way.

Who's Really Interested in Productivity? (I Mean, Really?)

WE'RE FREQUENTLY ASKED, "How can I enlist other people around me to hop on board with this approach to getting things done? It's so simple, and it would make our life, work, and relationships so much easier!" This is often accompanied by an unspoken frustration: "Look, *I* see the value of implementing this—why don't *they*?!"

> Knowledge must come through action; you can have no test which is not fanciful, save by trial.
>
> —SOPHOCLES

Why do some people "get" this productivity-enhancing methodology and others not? Why are we as likely to have a fourteen-year-old student catch the spirit of the productivity principles as a CEO or a midmanager or a soccer mom? And why does one manager or CEO or soccer mom take to this while another one with the same kind of work and personality does not?

After twenty-plus years, I've been able to find only one common denominator among the people and the organizations that have most implemented our productivity methodologies: They have a consistent internal forward momentum. It's not lip-served or a merely conceptual "desire to improve" but rather a real deep-seated pull toward some improved future state for themselves or at least for things they feel responsible for. That's why people and organizations that look very similar have highly varying degrees of attraction to what we do. Their drive to get somewhere easier, faster, and better can be quite different.

Nothing is more revealing than movement.
—MARTHA GRAHAM

Here's the ongoing paradox: The people who need what we do the least are the people who use it the most. Why? Because they're already in the driver's seat and they're already in motion. Without a gut-level sense that you are ultimately in control of what's happening to you, you won't even consider the option that you could manage it better. And if you're not propelling yourself forward to some degree, you won't have any real reference points for wanting to do something different to make it "easier, faster, better," even if it kissed you on the face.

There is a simple, but not obvious, truth about productivity enhancement: If you aren't identified with getting someplace different from where you are (and with improving the quality of your experience in the process), you probably won't invest the energy to explore ways of doing things better.

A man who dares to waste one hour of time has not discovered the value of life.
—CHARLES DARWIN

You also have to be willing to admit that you might need to change some behaviors. If you're interested in making something happen and truly hate wasting resources or stressing yourself inordinately, you'll be open to and hungry to at least explore best practices you may not yet know about.

The Formula I race teams spend thousands of hours and millions of dollars testing and installing the most minute of processes, systems, and behaviors that might give them a split-second edge when the chips are down. But if you don't think you're in a race, or don't care how good you can get at what you're doing, or don't really need to relieve your stress, then these kinds of investments would obviously be a waste of time and resources. Doing what you'd need to do to free up drag would *seem* a drag. Researching and sharpening processes will not always be the most strategic focus for high performers, but they'll always have their antennae tuned for such opportunities.

I don't think necessity is the mother of invention—invention, in my opinion, arises directly from idleness, possibly also from laziness. To save oneself trouble.

—AGATHA CHRISTIE

So don't be too discouraged if not everyone on your block buys into "What are we trying to accomplish here?" and "What's the next action?" as the operant questions of work. Don't be too surprised if your spouse or your boss or your assistant or your teenage son isn't particularly open to objectifying and managing all his or her commitments and communications seamlessly. You'll be sharing some common sense with them, for sure, but, for many of them, you might as well be from Mars.

We are working toward the goal that these thought processes will one day be modeled, taught, and expected in our education system, from the get-go. Perhaps then they will be standard operating procedure for most everyone, and we'll all be into bigger and better problems and opportunities. Meanwhile, we'll be satisfied to support those who really want to take it and run with it.

By the way . . .

○ To what degree do you want things to be different for you eighteen months from now? Are you getting there as easily as you can?

○ To what extent do you think your systems, processes, or approaches could stand improvement?

51.

It's easier to move when you're in motion.

In karate, you quickly learn that when you're sparring with an opponent, you never stop moving. It's much easier to respond and move quickly—even when you need to go in the opposite direction—if you're already in motion. It takes much more effort to begin to move than to change direction. If you're positively engaged, with any part of your life, it is easier to deal with change and to get anything else done.

Overwhelmed? Take the Helm

WHEN I HAD my own sailboat, an old skipper gave me a great tip: "If someone's about to hurl," he said, "give 'em the helm." When you feel motion sickness, a key to eliminating queasiness is to focus on the horizon. It's even better to grab the wheel. I've never known anyone to get carsick while she was driving the car. A much deeper level of equilibrium is accessed when you actually take charge of a moving vessel.

> *What makes a river so restful to people is that it doesn't have any doubt—it is sure where it is going, and it doesn't want to go anywhere else.*
>
> —HAL BOYLE

The main reason you'll feel much better when you implement the methods of collecting, processing, organizing, and intuitively managing the total inventory of your work is not that it creates less to do. It's because it automatically puts you back in the driver's seat, at the center of your universe. You become cause instead of effect.

Overwhelm and overcommitment, though they seem to create so much stress these days, are not the real culprits. Many times, you'll actually thrive in those situations in which you're working "against all odds." Try single-handedly sailing out into the deep blue ocean—or merely getting out of bed some mornings!

Drive thy business, or it will drive thee.
—BENJAMIN FRANKLIN

When you're in an earthquake on a unicycle, juggling chain saws, the only way to survive is to tack down everything you can tack down, so you can deal with what you can't.
—STEPHEN CHAKWIN

The angst arises when you let loose the reins and stop directing your own energy. Indeed, we are all at the mercy of things bigger than ourselves, and at some point we all learn that surrendering to—and cooperating with—some greater and larger aspect of the universe is the real game. That kind of letting go is actually a positive and highly directed energy, not at all the kind of caving-in experience of being victimized by the voluminous details of your life.

Avoiding things that demand your attention is like trying to stop the boat from rocking. Answering "What's your desired outcome?" and "What's the next action?"—even about the pieces of paper on your desk—puts you back at the helm.

By the way . . .
○ When you don't know what to do, what are some really good things to do?

52.

The biggest successes come from the most failures.

Missiles and rockets are off course most of the time they're in the air. They get where they're going because they continually course-correct. You make mistakes only in a game you're playing. Play a game you can win, and lose as much as you need to, to get there.

The Year of Better Choices

ONE OF MY HEALTHIEST moments of awareness came recently when I realized that I was going to measure my progress as a human being not by any specific success or failure but by the percentage of better choices I will make over time.

I decided that this was going to be my Year of Better Choices—and hoped that every year thereafter would be as well. How often do I choose to exercise, even when I don't feel like it? Or to be of service to someone else, when I don't have time? Or to be strategic instead of simply busy? Or to focus on something creative and inspirational instead of pandering to my less noble impulses? Or to be frugal instead of lavish? Or lavish instead of frugal?

Thousands of people have talent. I might as well congratulate you for having eyes in your head. The one and only thing that counts is: Do you have staying power?
—NOËL COWARD

I've read that we have fifty thousand thoughts a day (how did anyone count them?!). Whatever the number may be, each is an opportunity for choosing what thought to have. Or at least what thought to *continue* to have. I don't blame myself for having the thought "What if I get run over by a bus?" My challenge is, Do I continue to focus on it?

We are all, it seems, saving ourselves for the Senior Prom. But many of us forget that somewhere along the way we must learn to dance.

—ALAN
HARRINGTON

I know that I won't always make the best choice. And every time I don't, it's a perfect opportunity to write myself off as the lowest slug of the universe, undeserving of anything good ever again in my life. I have made *that* self-limiting choice too many times. Too often we set ourselves up for our own version of win/lose. We get up to bat and miss the ball, then beat ourselves up for not being any good at baseball. And we check out of the game.

Aim for success, not perfection. Never give up your right to be wrong, because then you will lose the ability to learn new things and move forward with your life. Remember that fear always lurks behind perfectionism. Confronting your fears and allowing yourself the right to be human can, paradoxically, make you a far happier and more productive person.

—DR. DAVID M.
BURNS

Some of our clients with whom we have spent quality time installing new and effective work behaviors feel guilty when they don't "keep the process going" as they know they "should." Because our methods are so simple and common-sense based, they think they should have "gotten" them all instantly and that this should be an installed practice from which they will never waver. So when they do slip off the wagon, they may feel like just giving up their progress toward the higher ground of maximum productivity. "If I can't make something so easy work immediately and all the time, why bother trying?"

Years ago, I had a great golf instructor who said, "Don't worry about your score or the balls that went in the water. Just know that every time you play, you'll hit more great shots!" Good advice. So this year I'm making at least a few more great shots than last. That attitude keeps me in the game and getting better at it.

When you stop reading this, you will choose what to focus on and what to do next. Take your swing. You might really connect. And if you don't, don't worry. You'll have a lot more chances before you go to sleep tonight.

By the way . . .

○ Name three games in life you've gotten better at. What's another one you might like to start playing?

○ Have you made a big enough mistake lately?

PART V

REMIND YOURSELF OF THE FUNDAMENTALS

or

Common Sense Isn't That Common

Being ready for anything requires the facility to get things done, effectively and efficiently. You get things done by defining "done" and deciding what "doing" would look like. But because the actual volume and complexity of the inventory of things we deal with in life is so huge, it's handy to have some guides to follow for a consistent model to apply for getting your arms around it all. For a complete elucidation of the following best practices, read *Getting Things Done: The Art of Stress-Free Productivity* (Viking, 2001).

The Five Phases of Workflow Mastery

This is the guide to gaining "horizontal" control—how to capture, identify, and manage your total inventory of commitments. Stages 2 and 3 are further elucidated in the Processing and Organizing Workflow diagram (page 160), which is a great tool to keep in front of you at your desk, until the procedure is totally habitual.

1. Collect

○ Capture anything and everything that has your attention in leakproof external "buckets" (your in-baskets, e-mail, notebooks, voice mail, etc.) to get them out of your short-term memory.

○ Have as few of these collectors as you can and as many as you need.

○ Empty them regularly, by processing and organizing (see next guide).

2. Process

○ Process the items you have collected (decide about your collected stuff).

○ If it is not actionable, toss it, "tickle" it for possible later action, or file it as reference.

○ If it is actionable, decide the very next physical action, which you do (if less than two minutes), delegate (and track on waiting-for list), or defer (put on an action-reminder list or in an action folder). If one action will not close the loop, then identify the commitment as a project and put it on a reminder list of projects.

3. Organize

○ Group the results of processing your input into appropriately retrievable and reviewable categories. The four key action categories are:
  - Projects (projects you have commitments to finish)
  - Calendar (actions that must occur on a specific day or time)
  - Next Actions (actions to be done as soon as possible)
  - Waiting For (projects and actions others are supposed to be doing, which you care about)

○ Add subcategories of these lists if it makes them easier to use (Calls, Errands, At Home, At Computer, etc.).

○ Add lists of longer-horizon goals and values that influence you.

○ Add checklists that may be useful as needed (job description, event trigger lists, org charts, etc.).

○ Maintain a general-reference filing system for information and materials that have no action but need to be retrievable.

○ Maintain an on-hold system for triggers of possible actions at later dates (someday / maybe lists, calendar, tickler).

○ Maintain support-information files for projects as needed (can be kept in reference system or in pending area).

4. Review

○ Review calendar and action lists daily (or whenever you could possibly do any of them).

○ Conduct a customized weekly review to clean up, update, maintain, and advance your systems. (see Weekly Review, page 163).

○ Review the longer-horizon lists of goals, values, and visions as often as required to keep your project list complete and current.

5. Do

○ Make choices about your actions based upon what you can do (context), how much time you have, how much energy you have, and then your priorities.

○ Stay flexible by maintaining a "total life" action-reminder system, always accessible for review, trusting your intuition in moment-to-moment decision making.

○ Ensure the best intuitive choices by consistent, regular focus on priorities ("What is the value to me of doing X instead of doing Y?"). Revisit and recalibrate your commitments at appropriate intervals for the various levels of life and work:

- Runway—current actions (daily)
- 10,000 feet—current projects (weekly)
- 20,000 feet—current responsibilities (monthly)
- 30,000 feet—one-to-two-year goals (quarterly)
- 40,000 feet—three-to-five-year goals (annually)
- 50,000+ feet—career, purpose, lifestyle (annually+)

Processing and Organizing Workflow

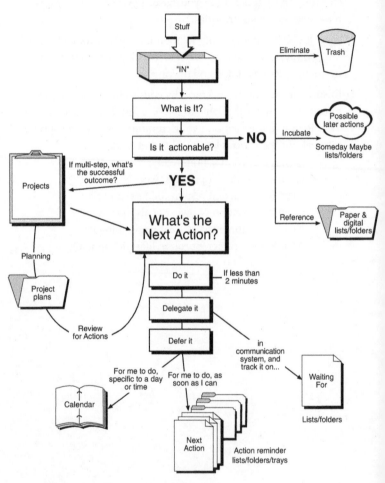

The Natural Planning Model

This model is based upon the way your brain naturally plans anything. It provides "vertical" control, i.e., the most effective way to think through a single and specific project or situation. Once you've identified all your projects, any one of them may require more focus at one or more of these levels for you to feel comfortable about it.

1. Purpose/Guiding Principles

○ Why is this being done? What would "on purpose" really mean?

○ What are the key standards to hold in making decisions and acting on this project? What rules do we play by?

○ The purpose and principles are the guiding criteria for making decisions on the project.

2. Mission/Vision/Goal/Successful Outcome

○ What would it be like if it were totally successful? How would I know?

○ What would that success look or feel like for each of the parties with an interest?

3. Brainstorming

○ What are all the things that occur to me about this? What is the current reality?

○ What do I know? What do I not know? What ought I consider? What haven't I considered? Etc.

○ Be complete, open, and nonjudgmental, and resist critical analysis.

○ View from all sides.

4. Organizing

o Identify components (subprojects), sequences, and/or priorities.

o Create outlines, bulleted lists, or organizing charts as needed for review and control.

5. Next Actions

o Determine next actions on current independent components. (What should be done next, and who will do it?)

o If more planning is required, determine the next action to accomplish that.

If needed, shift the level of focus on the project as follows:

· If your project needs more clarity, raise the level of your focus (e.g., move from actions back to plans, plans back to brainstorming, vision back to purpose).

· If your project needs more to be happening, lower the level of your focus (e.g., move from vision to brainstorming, from plans to actions).

How much planning is required?

· If the project is off your mind, your planning is sufficient. If it's still on your mind, keep applying the model until it's clear.

The Weekly Review

The first challenge is to implement these models, and the second is to keep them active and functional. This guide provides the master key to achieving a consistently more relaxed and productive style of life and work. This process, whenever it's done, facilitates executive command-center thinking and confidence, and it's most effective when it's practiced every seven days.

Loose Papers

○ Gather all scraps of paper, business cards, receipts, and miscellaneous paper. Put into your in-basket to process.

Process Your Notes

○ Review any journal/notes types of entries, meeting notes, and miscellaneous notes scribbled on notebook paper. Decide and enter action items, projects, waiting-fors, etc., as appropriate.

Empty Your Head

○ Put in writing (in appropriate categories) any new projects, action items, waiting-fors, someday/maybes, etc., not yet captured.

Review Action Lists

○ Mark off completed actions. Review for reminders of further action steps to record.

Review Waiting-For List

○ Record appropriate actions for any needed follow-up. Check off received ones.

Review Project (and Larger Outcome) Lists

○ Evaluate status of projects, goals and outcomes, one by one, ensuring at least one current action item on each. Browse through work-in-progress support material to trigger new actions, completions, waiting-fors, etc.

Review Previous Calendar Data

○ Review past calendar in detail for remaining action items, reference data, etc., and transfer into the active system.

Review Upcoming Calendar

○ Review upcoming calendar events—long and short term. Capture actions triggered.

Review Any Relevant Checklists

○ Use as a trigger for any new actions.

Review Someday/Maybe List

○ Review for any projects that may now have become active, and transfer to projects list. Delete items no longer of interest.

Be Creative and Courageous

○ Any new, wonderful, harebrained, creative, thought-provoking, risk-taking ideas to add into your system???

Afterword

UNEXPECTED CHANGE seems here to stay, so I look forward to the further development and distribution of these ideas and techniques for mastering the game of work and the business of life. I invite your feedback and participation.

These and similar themes continue to be explored through our regular newsletters. A free subscription is available through our Web site (www.davidco.com, which also has additional free material about productivity) or by e-mailing us at customerservice@davidco.com.

I wish you all the best.

Ready?

David Allen